Discipline and Learning:

An Inquiry into Student-Teacher Relationships

National Education Association
Washington, D.C..

Previously published material used in this book may use the pronoun "he" to denote an abstract individual, e.g., "the student." We have not attempted to alter this material, although we currently use "she/he" in such instances.

—NEA Publishing

Library of Congress Cataloging in Publication Data
Main entry under title:

Discipline and learning.

  Includes bibliographical references.
  CONTENTS: Wickersham, P. H. The first encounter.—
Cooper, J. E. The nature and purpose of discipline.—
Montessori, M. Montessori on youth and children. [etc.]
  1. School discipline—Addresses, essays, lectures.
2. Classroom management—Addresses, essays, lectures.
3. Teacher-student relationships—Addresses, essays,
lectures. I. National Education Association of the
United States.
LB3013.D57   371.5   75-2042
ISBN 0-8106-1349-2

Contents

Introduction

Discipline and learning—the two words seem to have strikingly different meanings, but if we think about them we realize that they are integrally related. Discipline is necessary for learning, and effective learning is a form of discipline. Indeed in some ways the two words cannot be separated, and we tend to accept the maxim that good curriculum and good discipline are the same thing.

Today discipline is acknowledged as one of the most pressing concerns of the community at large. There is still disagreement, however, about what kinds of behavior merit disciplinary action. Along with our recognition of the rights of all individuals, no matter what age or role in society, has come the vivid practical awareness that the inconsiderate exercise of these rights may infringe on the rights of others. The student who whispers in a corner of a room in which other students are trying to read silently is running the risk of disturbing the learning process for the other students. At the opposite extreme, those students who commit acts of physical violence against students or teachers are taking disruptive behavior into the realm of crime, which ultimately must be dealt with by the community at large. In any case, when disruptive behavior becomes a community problem the schools are criticized for misplaced values or failure to accept and carry out responsibility. And teachers find the blame directed toward them.

Our notions of the purpose of discipline have changed radically over two hundred years. At one time it was thought essential to aid memory with corporal punishment such as whipping. We, on the other hand, view corporal punishment as an infringement of the rights of students and a denial of respect for the individual. Indeed the NEA Task Force on Corporal Punishment found that this method of discipline is completely ineffectual. In spite of the change in attitude toward punishment, however, many teachers' feelings about what constitutes disruptive behavior have remained fairly constant over the past half century.

This book offers the classroom teacher some approaches to the general topic of discipline from a historical perspective as well as the contemporary point of view. It discusses punishment and order and justice, and it shows teachers ways to approach the more serious problems attached to maintaining good discipline in the classroom, as well as ways of helping students arrive at self-discipline. It is hoped that these selections will aid the reader in achieving greater effectiveness in day-to-day classroom instruction by bringing an increased awareness and knowledge to the practical management of discipline. Learning can only take place in an environment that reflects the care of the teacher for all the students—and that care means not only the concern for their personal welfare, but also the establishment and maintenance of good discipline.

5

Discipline

The First Encounter

Philip H. Wickersham
Slippery Rock State College

Did you ever wonder why it is that:

— professors who lecture to you about learning theory, never use that theory themselves?

— students are engaged in the grand game of telling professors what they want to hear?

— the assumption is made that if you know something, you can teach it to others?

— students haven't the backbone to walk out of classes that are neither stimulating nor informative?

— the lecture system, instituted in Medieval times when books were relatively scarce so that teachers had to disseminate and interpret for students, is the primary technique used in the twentieth century?

— if students were given a choice between required courses and areas of interest, many classrooms would be empty?

— professors who decry educating for an elite group are hell bent on making either the Ph.D. degree or the Ed.D. degree (depending on which they hold) the more prestigious?

— teachers administer tests and children submit to them, each knowing full well the perpetration of fraud. If you don't believe it, try giving a test without announcing it in advance. We both know what the results will be. We also know what would happen if the same test were given six months hence.

— those who write profusely on innovation in the schools do so little of it themselves?

— with all of the knowledge we have about the effect of child rearing practices, the matter is still left largely to chance? Is this knowledge

News of Pi Chapter (Phi Delta Kappa), University of Illinois, Urbana, December 11, 1968, P. H. Wickersham, T. A. Auger, R. Grandchamp, editors, vol. 33, no. 2.

any less important or crucial than how to solve quadratic equations?
— your *fear* of the grade prevents you from enrolling in courses in areas that would broaden, not confine, your interests?
— something happens to that curiosity and wonder so natural in the early grades? Observe those same children in college preparatory programs.
— the skills needed to get you through college are not congruent with those needed to function as a competent practitioner?
— qualifying examinations, don't?
— the following expression is held to be true?

teaching = understanding = lecturing = testing

— there is manifest unrest among students today? Perhaps we ought to be listening to what they have to say—or is that unreasonable?

The Nature and Purpose of Discipline

John E. Cooper
Parsons College

A Changing View of Discipline

Discipline in the past meant subjection of the individual to control—control of the weak to the will of the strong. Control resided in the personal authority of the teacher and the parent over the child, the priest over the parishoner, the officer over the private, and the master over the slave. Individuals were "disciplined" in additional ways by the impersonal force of law, custom, and social opinion.

The importance of control should continue to receive recognition in newer concepts of discipline. In the development of free men, however, now a different kind of control is emphasized as an outgrowth of the application of democratic ideals to social behavior. This is control which the individual imposes upon himself in recognition of his obligations to others and to himself. External control must continue to be accessible to authority as a reminder to the immature who tend to be forgetful and as a deterrent to the lawless who would jeopardize the welfare of others for their own selfish purposes.

In the schools of the past, discipline was viewed as subjection of the will of the individual and of the class to the teacher. Through obedience, instruction became possible; the exercise of discipline provided a means for achieving the educational objectives of the teacher.[1] History reveals that many teachers turned to harsh "disciplinary methods" in attempting to attain these objectives—in many instances because learning experiences, teaching methods, and instructional materials were alien to the abilities and interests of rebellious children. The reader may find it useful to distinguish some of the concepts which continue to adhere to the term *discipline:*

---

[1]Willard S. Elsbree and Harold J. McNally, *Elementary School Administration and Supervision* (New York: American Book Company, 1959), pp. 350-356.

Excerpted with permission from *The Elementary School Principalship* by John E Cooper. © 1967 by Charles E. Merrill Publishing Company. All rights reserved. Reprinted with permission.

11

1. *Punishment*, actual or threatened, may be necessary in order to achieve control, but it should not be confused with discipline itself.
2. *Control* is an aspect of discipline, but the primary source of control may be *internal* as well as *external* to the individual.
3. The best form of control is internal and is exercised voluntarily as the individual acknowledges its need. This is the exercise of *self-discipline,* a characteristic of personal maturity.
4. *Self-discipline* is revealed in the pursuit of a task which may not be rewarding immediately but is recognized by the individual to be a source of future satisfaction.

The Relation of Discipline to Teaching and Learning

Poor discipline habits, whether as unsatisfactory responses to internal or external influences, impede learning. The modern teacher understands the importance of order to learning, but order no longer can be regarded as a condition of pin-quiet silence to be maintained throughout the day. Order without pupil understanding of the objectives sought and the methods permitted is a sterile accomplishment. Understanding of purpose and of acceptable behavior should be shared with children.

The productivity of a particular learning incident cannot be evaluated adequately by means of a noise meter. Some learning situations require students to be quiet, as in the listening phase of a music appreciation lesson. Others call for controlled noise, as when five committees are meeting simultaneously in the same classroom. Pupils, and occasionally teachers, require help in examining the relationship between noise from talking and the objectives of a particular learning activity.

As children become more aware of what they are seeking and how to proceed in attaining it, they become better able to adjust their behavior to cope with the requirements of a learning task. The result is growth toward self-discipline. Self-discipline, then, while a means to better learning, is also a desirable educational goal in its own right. One valid test of an effective curriculum is the extent to which learning experiences elicit a rich diversity of desirable responding behaviors on the part of pupils.

The Relationship of Discipline to Citizenship

Behavior which the student imposes upon himself for his own good and for the benefit of those around him is evidence of growth toward responsible membership in a free society. The American school has been given the increasingly difficult responsibility of preparing youth to meet the problems and challenges of accepting such membership. The school's task in citizenship education is more difficult than in the past because it must work with all children, not just a select sample. In addition, the school today is concerned with more than intellectual development; it is concerned with any aspect of behavior or development which affects the way the child relates to himself and to others. The work of the school has been made more difficult, also, by social change affecting life on a large scale.

As people live in increasingly close contact, the need for recognition of personal accountability increases. There is sad evidence that many adults have distorted the inescapable relationship which unites freedom and responsibility. Freedom is an elusive dream so long as responsibility goes begging.

The need for self-discipline continues to grow in proportion to the decreasing regulatory influence of the work day. Greater amounts of leisure time and a longer life in retirement open up to each person new vistas of freedom. They also pose the need for responsible behavior. The fate of a free society may rest upon the ability of individuals to choose and to use time for self-actualizing experiences rather than for vacuous or damaging ones.

One facet of the increasing degree of complexity and mobility of life is the requirement to meet new demands. The child in school needs to learn what behavior is appropriate in each of a variety of life situations. As he grows and his experiences broaden, the child is thrust into new roles, each possessing unique behavioral expectations. The school must help the child to understand and to judge these sets of cultural demands for intelligent participation in society. The elementary principal who is cognizant of this problem will assist children, teachers, and parents to understand such powerful value influencers as television, motion pictures, and newspapers.

How, then, can the elementary school best affect those impressionable years of a child so that he grows toward individual and social responsibility? Certainly anarchy in the classroom—even though it is perpetrated in the name of democracy—is not the answer. The immature require controls for their own safety and for the process of education to take place. In the education of the young the burden of control must be retained by adult leadership. Sound work habits must be instilled if children are to become skilled in the use of such essential cultural tools as reading, problem-solving, listening, speaking, and criticizing.

> The tools should remain tools, however. They should not become ends in themselves. Techniques are necessary to keep cultural traditions alive. They are not in themselves, however, the spark which lights the flame. It is important that work habits be established, but if they become habits only, the work for which they should serve becomes meaningless—culture deteriorates into mechanical civilization.[2]

One critical discrimination facing the teacher concerned with the relationship of self-discipline to effective citizenship is the problem of pupil needs versus pupil wishes. Adult wisdom is needed at this point if

[2]Katherine Maria Wolf, *The Controversial Problem of Discipline* (New York: Child Study Association of America, 1953), p. 19.

the teacher is to avoid the undesirable possibilities of too much authority on the one hand and negligence on the other. The judgment of a child is not a reliable guide at this point. His wishes may run contrary to his needs. In fact, he may neither be aware of nor understand his needs.

In his thought-provoking book, *Progressive Education at the Crossroads*, Boyd Bode offers educators some helpful ideas in resolving this problem. He advises that conflicting desires should be brought to the court of long-range programs to be settled. The school's program should be used to identify those needs which are relevant.

> Unless we assume that there is a predestined end for human living and that we are in the know as to what this end is, there is no justification whatsoever for talking so blithely about needs. An authoritarian scheme of education could make excellent use of a doctrine of needs, for it would be in a position to know at every point what it was talking about. In a democratic system of education the situation is entirely different. We cannot start with needs, because needs must be determined with reference to the way of life which the pupil eventually adopts as his own and the choice that he will make cannot be presupposed from the outset. Instead of using needs as a starting point, we educate people in order that they may discover their needs.[3]

According to Bode, the central concern of American schools should be democracy versus tradition. In light of his position, this issue becomes the basic need of organized education to which all other needs are subordinated.

While the teacher of the immature may have to exert most of the controls needed to bring order to learning, she cannot afford to lose sight of the desirability of giving children an increasing determination in setting their own standards. She will provide opportunities for initiative, decision-making, and the acceptance of responsibility as evidence is forthcoming of their ability to receive it. To do less through omission or commission is an inexcusable neglect in the preparation of the young for the demands of life in a democracy. The cultivation of the free mind cannot proceed adequately by training methods better adapted for making obedient vassals to serve a Gestapo state.

---

[3]Boyd H. Bode, *Progressive Education at the Crossroads* (New York: Newson and Company, 1938), pp. 69-70.

Montessori on Youth and Children

Excerpted from the writings of Maria Montessori

Youth

Respect for young people is essential. One must never treat adolescents as children. They have passed that stage. It is of greater value to treat them as if their worth were superior to their real worth than to minimize their merits and risk injury to their sense of personal dignity.

The young must be left with sufficient liberty to act according to individual initiative. Let us, then, prepare the means while leaving them the liberty to create. But, in order that individual action be simultaneously free and fruitful, it must be confined within certain limits and obey certain rules which constitute the necessary direction. The limits and rules must be observed by the entire institution. One must not give the adolescents the impression that they are not conscientious, that they are unable to discipline themselves.

The rules, like the materials for the youngest children, must be "necessary and sufficient" to maintain order and assure progress. The organization must be conceived in such a way that the adolescents do not feel in any way out of place as a consequence, and so that they may adapt in any surroundings.

The adaptation will then manifest itself by "collaboration," source of the social harmony which accelerates individual progress.

The surroundings ought to make "free choice" easy. But it is necessary to guide the child so that he does not waste his time and energy in aimless activity.

From the set of these preparations will arise not only discipline but also the proof that discipline is an aspect of individual liberty, an essential factor of success in life.

Reprinted by permission of Schocken Books, Inc., from *From Childhood to Adolescence* by Maria Montessori. Copyright © 1948 by Maria Montessori. Copyright © 1958 by Desclée de Brouwer. Copyright © 1973 by Schocken Books, Inc.

Children

Discipline must come through liberty. Here is a great principle which is difficult for followers of common-school methods to understand. How shall one obtain *discipline* in a class of free children? Certainly in our system, we have a concept of discipline very different from that commonly accepted. If discipline is founded upon liberty, the discipline itself must necessarily be *active*. We do not consider an individual disciplined only when he has been rendered as artificially silent as a mute and as immovable as a paralytic. He is an individual *annihilated*, not *disciplined*.

We call an individual disciplined when he is master of himself, and can, therefore, regulate his own conduct when it shall be necessary to follow some rule of life. Such a concept of *active discipline* is not easy either to comprehend or to apply. But certainly it contains a great *educational* principle, very different from the old-time absolute and undiscussed coercion to immobility.

* * *

The first dawning of real discipline comes through work. At a given moment it happens that a child becomes keenly interested in a piece of work, showing it by the expression of his face, by his intense attention, by his perseverance in the same exercise. That child has set foot upon the road leading to discipline. Whatever be his undertaking—an exercise for the senses, an exercise in buttoning up or lacing together, or washing dishes—it is all one and the same.

Children, who are undertaking something for the first time are extremely slow. Their life is governed in this respect by laws especially different from ours. Little children accomplish slowly and perseveringly, various complicated operations agreeable to them, such as dressing, undressing, cleaning the room, washing themselves, setting the table, eating, etc. In all this they are extremely patient, overcoming all the difficulties presented by an organism still in process of formation. But we, on the other hand, noticing that they are "tiring themselves out" or "wasting time" in accomplishing something which we would do in a moment and without the least effort, put ourselves in the child's place and do it ourselves. Always with the same erroneous idea, that the end to be obtained is the completion of the action, we dress and wash the child, we snatch out of his hands objects which he loves to handle, we pour the soup into his bowl, we feed him, we set the table for him. And after such services, we consider him with that injustice always practised by those who domineer over others even with benevolent intentions, to be incapable and inept. We often speak of him as "impatient" simply because we are not patient enough to allow his actions to follow laws of time differing from our own; we call him "tyrannical" exactly because we employ tyranny towards him. This stain, this false imputation, this calumny on childhood has become an integral part of the theories concerning childhood, in reality so patient and gentle.

The child, like every strong creature fighting for the right to live, rebels against whatever offends that occult impulse within him which is the voice of nature, and which he ought to obey; and he shows by violent actions, by screaming and weeping that he has been overborne and forced away from his mission in life. He shows himself to be a rebel, a revolutionist, an iconoclast, against those who do not understand him and who, fancying that they are helping him, are really pushing him backward in the highway of life. Thus even the adult who loves him, rivets about his neck another calumny, confusing his defence of his molested life with a form of innate naughtiness characteristic of little children.

A Memory Aid

Richard S. Uhrbrock

Professor Emeritus of Psychology, Ohio University

Historical Documents furnish examples of corporal punishment. The incident below illustrates how one man thought that by beating an innocent boy, he could reinforce the child's memory of the time and place of a particular historical occurrence:

On May 27, 1872, at the Cone Hotel, Crisfield, Maryland, John Marshall appeared before Virginia Commissioners who had been appointed to ascertain the boundary line between Maryland and Virginia. He testified, "I am going in my 63rd year ever since the 19th of the present month of May. I was born on Sykes Island. I came to Smith's Island to reside when I was about 17 years of age, and have resided on Smith's Island ever since. [Reference to boundary stone] Old Mr. William Tyler, when he and I were alone, he showed me a boundary stone . . . he told me that he was carried to that stone and whipped by his grandfather, I think named Butler Tyler, to the best of my knowledge, and that he was whipped there to make him remember that it was a boundary stone between the two states."

Report and accompanying documents of Virginia Commissioners, etc. Richmond: Dept. Public Printing, 1873, p. 173.

What Behavior Problems Do Teachers Regard as Serious?

Puran L. Rajpal

Assistant Professor of Education
State Univ. College, Fredonia, N.Y.

A Comparison: 1928 and 1972

Fifty behavior problems listed by E. K. Wickman in 1928* were recently rated according to their seriousness by 100 teachers of grades 3-6 and by 20 permanently certified school psychologists assigned to elementary schools of Western New York. Both groups filled out a questionnaire which asked the question: "How serious (or undesirable) is this behavior in any elementary school boy?" Responses were made for the 50 behaviors on a seven-point grading scale and the results for each group.

---

*E. K. Wickman, *Children's Behavior Problems and Teachers' Attitudes.* New York: The Commonwealth Fund, 1928, p. 247.

Reprinted with permission From *Phi Delta Kappan*, May 1972. © 1972 by Phi Delta Kappa, Inc. All rights reserved.

Table 1

Rank-Order of 50 Behavior Problems, Based on Ratings Made by Four Groups: Rankings of Teachers and School Psychologists in This Study in Comparison with Rankings of Wickman's Teachers and Mental Hygienists in 1928

Behavior Items	Wickman Teachers	Teachers in This Study	Wickman Mental Hygienists	School Psychologists in This Study
Tardiness	30	38	43	39.5
Truancy	6	5	23	17.5
Destroying school materials	10	3	45	.4
Untruthfulness (lying)	5	4	23	10.5
Imaginative lying	42	28	33	34
Cheating	9	6	23	8.5
Stealing	2	1	13.5	4
Profanity	15	34.5	47	44.5
Smoking	18	34.5	49	46.5
Obscene notes, pictures, talk	4	23	28.5	34
Masturbation	3	45	41	46.5
Heterosexual activity	1	32.5	26	36
Disorderliness	20.5	46	46	44.5
Whispering and note writing	46.5	50	50	50
Interrupting (talkativeness)	43.5	48	48	49
Restlessness (overactivity)	49	47	41	42.5
Inattention	26	20	34	20
Lack of interest in work	14	14	25	8.5
Carelessness in work	24.5	24	37.5	24
Laziness	16.5	18	35.5	16
Unreliableness (irresponsible)	12	8	21	10.5
Disobedience	11	17	41	20
Impertinence (defiance)	7	21.5	37.5	28.5
Cruelty and bullying	8	7	6	4
Quarrelsomeness	27	21.5	31	25.5
Tattling	46.5	42	28.5	39.5
Stubbornness (contrariness)	32.5	43	20	39.5
Sullenness (sulkiness)	35	27	12	22
Temper tantrums	13	13	17	14.5
Impudence, impoliteness, rudeness	16.5	19	32	28.5
Selfishness (unsportsmanship)	24.5	15	16	12
Domineering, overbearing	32.5	26	11	25.5
Shyness (bashfulness)	50	39	13.5	34
Sensitiveness	48	29.5	10	23
Unsocial, withdrawing	40.5	9	1	1
Overcritical of others	45	29.5	9	27
Thoughtlessness (forgetting)	38	32.5	39	32
Inquisitiveness, meddlesomeness	43.5	44	44	39.5
Silliness (smartness)	39	49	30	48
Unhappy, depressed	22.5	2	3	2
Resentful	29	12	4	7
Nervousness	20.5	16	18.5	14.5
Fearfulness	36	11	5	6
Enuresis	19	36.5	27	20
Dreaminess	40.5	41	18.5	37
Slovenly in appearance	34	36.5	35.5	42.5
Suspiciousness	37	25	2	17.5
Physical coward	31	40	15	30.5
Easily discouraged	22.5	10	7	13
Suggestibility	28	31	8	30.5

Regulating Student Behavior Without Ending Up In Court

Edward T. Ladd

The late Dr. Ladd was Professor of Education
Emory University, Atlanta

How we got into the present dilemma and how we should
proceed to get out of it

Administrators of our public schools face a dilemma today which
they've never faced before: how to regulate student behavior without
being sued for violating students' rights or, if sued, without being
overruled in court. For at least a century, of course, lawsuits have been
brought on behalf of students whom school officials have beaten,
suspended, or expelled. Only recently, though, has the practice
become so common as to play a serious part in teachers' or administrators' day-to-day disciplinary decisions. Now there are many
school districts where, when a student subjected to disciplinary action
hauls the would-be discipliner into court, it no longer comes as a
surprise.

In the past four or five years, school officials who have suspended
students for "misconduct" have been sued on the ground that the
suspension was improper because the charge is unconstitutionally
vague. Officials have been sued because they have punished students
for demonstrating against school policies, disobeying principals'
orders or advocating disobedience, failing to stand during the Pledge
of Allegiance, publishing obscene materials, repeatedly violating no-
smoking rules, and ripping up a flag. Measures taken to enforce dress
and haircut rules that had been taken for granted since time im-
memorial have been attacked literally dozens of times in federal court.
The searching of school lockers without a warrant has been challenged
all the way to the Supreme Court. While teachers have hit students
who have displeased them ever since the first public schools opened
over three centuries ago, there are no parents who go to court charg-
ing that *any* use of physical violence against students is cruel and unusual, and hence illegal. Students given disciplinary transfers from
one school to another have sued to block such transfers on the ground

that they were decided upon without formal due process, that is, that the students were not presented with charges, allowed to bring witnesses, afforded impartial review, and the like. Students suspended for obvious and flagrant breaches have sued on the same ground.

In many of these cases the school officials have won, but in many others they have lost. Courts have placed administrators under almost unprecedented restrictions, and in at least one recent case a court punished an administrator for a disciplinary action by awarding the student damages.

All this is fairly widely known. What is less well known is that the new situation it has created goes strongly counter to a tradition which is basic to American public school administration and threatens what most conscientious administrators have always been taught to believe is good professional practice. Being an administrator trying to keep order in school must sometimes seem like being a modern physician trying to practice medicine in a country which has outlawed scalpels and hypodermic needles. The new restrictions put great demands on administrators' time and energy, too. The Topeka school district reported in 1970 to the Kansas legislature that giving students due process to the extent required by a new state law put a heavy burden of paper work on the schools, cost money the school district couldn't afford, took an average of four and a half hours of staff time per student suspended, and called for legal training that school officials didn't have. No wonder that a number of the New York City principals are retiring early and blaming their quitting on the New York Civil Liberties Union's Student Rights Project.

There is every reason to believe that in the years ahead the pressure will not lessen but increase. Even our present national concern about law and order will not halt the decades-old trend toward a strengthening of individual liberties. Nor is there an end in sight to young Americans' new-found disposition to sue in court. They seem almost to have become like the Englishmen described in *The Pickwick Papers:* When a principal crosses them, they instinctively cry, "I'll sue him!"

Besides, there is now money to support students' suits in amounts there never was before. Legal Aid Societies have become noticeably more active in this field. The American Civil Liberties Union and its affiliates around the country, though their litigation budgets are small, are many times busier in the field than just 10 years ago. But, much the most important, there are many antipoverty legal service organizations going to bat very aggressively for what they believe to be the rights of children and adolescents living in poverty. At a dozen universities around the country there are research and service centers backing up the antipoverty lawyers, and some of them are especially interested in broadening the legal rights of public school students. The National Juvenile Law Center at St. Louis University has already drafted a model statute to govern high school suspensions and expulsions (at the request, by the way, of the California Rural Legal Assistance office, an antipoverty agency). The Harvard Center for

Law and Education peddles a "Student Rights Litigation Kit," comments on proposed legislation, and points out new hills to be stormed. Last year its director, David Kirp, wrote:

> The public school system punishes poor children for being poor . . . . It offers them no say in the running of their schools, suspending those who dare to challenge the educational regime . . . . [This] punishment . . . is not inevitable . . . . Legal challenges are possible, and may even be successful.

But if the money for lawsuits against school officials comes from outside the educational establishment, some of those inside it are contributing ammunition in the form of ideas and documents. A little booklet published in 1969 by the National Association of Secondary School Principals (*The Reasonable Exercise of Authority*) has been read and quoted by students and civil liberties lawyers across the country. A much stronger code of student rights and responsibilities, adopted by the National Education Association in 1971, is adding to the pressure. Liberal codes of students' rights adopted by New York City, Philadelphia, Seattle, and many other systems are being examined by students and lawyers in dozens of other cities, as are liberal quasi-judicial rulings from the state school commissioners of New York and New Jersey. Finally, a few professors of education are getting into the act, teaching and writing about students' rights, and even serving as expert witnesses in court challenges to school practice.

School officials can expect, then, to come under attack for many more of the restrictions they commonly put on students' freedom. They may, for example, find themselves sued for requiring passes for trips through the hallways, insisting that students stay on campus during the school day, insisting on silence in lunchrooms, forbidding smoking, forbidding students to talk back to teachers and principals, requiring students to have conferences with counselors, requiring school newspaper editors to show their copy to faculty advisers, not allowing students to hold meetings at which no school official is present, making policy decisions without involving representatives of the students affected by them, and even for not allowing students who have been threatened to carry weapons in self-defense. The point is not that any of these restrictions are unjustified—or for that matter justified—but that any of them may quite possibly be challenged in court.

Furthermore, the practices school officials use for getting students to comply with requirements may also be challenged, such practices as insulting or abusing students, publicly humiliating them, being sarcastic, insisting on self-incriminating testimony, searching students' persons, keeping students after school when they have buses to catch or jobs to report to, recording alleged misbehavior in school records, and excluding students from extracurricular activities or student councils as a punishment. Counselors who tell disciplinary authorities about the content of confidential counseling sessions may likewise find themselves defendants in lawsuits. And so on and on.

A large part of the panoply of disciplinary requirements and practices is under fire and more of it may be soon. Not a little of it has already succumbed. Meanwhile, disorder in schools appears to increase.

This is a terrible dilemma. How are school administrators to deal with it—other than by retiring? There is a way, I believe. To find it, we must understand the dilemma's underlying causes, the forces in which today's administrators are tossed as if in a blanket. And to identify those forces we first must look at the rationale for the way authority and power are distributed and exercised in the typical school. In his important new book, *The Culture of the School and the Process of Change*, Seymour Sarason says that "in each classroom there is a constitution, verbalized or unverbalized, consistent or inconsistent . . . that governs behavior." We are concerned here with what could be called the constitution of the school. Because of its legal overtones, the term "constitution" is not a bad one; a still better one, perhaps, is "the system of governance."

To understand fully the system of governance that prevails in our public schools, it will be helpful to recall the system of governance in the community in which these schools were born and reared. The public school originated in Puritan Massachusetts, a colony that started out as a private, commercial corporation, controlled by a governor and 12 directors. The inner circle, having no confidence in the judgment of the members, kept the power tightly in their own hands. They claimed, indeed, that a higher authority had given them the sole right to "correct, govern, punish, pardon, and rule." Conscientiously, they endeavored to enforce conformity in all matters they believed to be of public concern, which encompassed the members' religion, private lives, and pleasures, including sexual behavior, flashy clothes, and long hair. Noncomformists were not allowed to run for office or even to vote. Newcomers who would swell the ranks of the community were welcome on condition that they accepted these arrangements and didn't try to rock the boat.

Discipline was simple and swift, and due process of law and opportunity for appeals hardly existed. Humiliating punishments, including corporal punishment, were routine, and brutal ones not out of the question. Members of the community who were anti-Establishment and spoke out unconventionally or insubordinately could be—and often were—expelled. The idea that some people were incorrigible and must simply be gotten rid of seems to have been a commonplace.

This was the governance system within which the "Old Deluder Satan" Act was passed. ("It being one of the chief projects of that old deluder Satan to keep men from the knowledge of the Scriptures . . . it is . . . ordered, that every township in this jurisdiction, after the Lord hath increased them to the number of 50 householders, shall then forthwith appoint one within their town to teach all such children as shall report to him to write and read.") From the marriage of Puritan religion and the Puritan state, then, emerged our original public schools. Notice four of the key principles of their common system of governance:

1. Those in authority get that authority from above, and it is essentially unlimited except by their obligations to higher authority and the laws created in its name.

2. Those in authority are fully responsible for seeing to it that those below them behave correctly in every respect.

3. Those at the bottom have few rights, largely nominal ones, and are forced to rely mainly on privileges extended to them when they have shown acceptable judgment and behavior.

4. Since those at the bottom cannot be counted on to embrace their role voluntarily, the system must provide for continuous intimidation, occasional coercion, and, as a last resort, removal.

What these four principles came to mean in the operation of our public schools and what they have meant over the intervening years requires no elaboration. While through the generations there has been a great broadening of the schools' gene pool, the traits of the original governance system are still apparent.

The Puritan community was also the setting in which the civil law dealing with public school discipline was born and nurtured. Most if not all of the early court decisions which became the precedents on this subject came from local and state courts in New England and particularly Massachusetts. A classic example is a seminal decision which directly or indirectly has influenced almost all the subsequent decisions in this area, that rendered in the case of *Hodgkins* v. *Rockport* in 1870:

> When a scholar is guilty of misconduct which injuriously affects the discipline and management of the school, we think the law vests in the [school] committee the power of determining whether the welfare of the school requires his exclusion . . . . If they exercise this power in good faith, their decision is not subject to review by the court.

That the Puritan concept remains strong in school law is suggested by the way school law specialists still commonly refer to the regulating of student conduct as "pupil control."

It is on the framework of the Puritan principles of governance that our great public school system has grown and flourished. These principles have repeatedly been sanctioned by local and state courts, and on occasion by legislatures. To judge from responses to the Harris and Gallup polls, which call for stricter discipline in the schools, they still command the support of a majority of the public. And they are a central element—often not even put into words—of the tradition in which school administrators have been trained, and which most conscientious, effective school administrators have tried to uphold. The legal problems surrounding discipline today come largely from attacks on these principles.

It is no mere chance that most student rights cases are brought in *federal* courts by lawyers arguing from the Bill of Rights, for federal courts and civil liberties lawyers represent in general a quite distinct and different system of governance. This system, also going far back into our history, indeed into the history of England, is the Madisonian system of governance embodied in our federal constitution and interpreted over the years by our federal courts. In it the rights of individuals, far from being left out, are central: *Everyone* has certain important rights, including the rights to freedom of speech and the press, to a degree of privacy, and to due process of law. These rights don't have to be earned; they don't hinge on the fulfilling of duties or obligations. Nor can they be taken away from anyone, no matter how irresponsible or stupid, how nonconformist or disruptive, he is. So central are rights, indeed, that duties and obligations are nothing more than means to the exercising of rights. Ultimate authority comes not from above but from below; it is not centralized but is scattered equally among the members of the community. Those who govern have defined functions beyond which they may not go. Since everyone else has *some* power, theirs is limited from all directions, and a special kind of impartial body, the court, exists to referee conflicts. To keep the system working, everyone must temper his respect for authority with a measure of continuous defensiveness and skepticism.

Madison himself summed up the key principles of this system when he wrote in *The Federalist, No. X:*

> As long as the reason of man continues fallible, and he is at liberty to exercise it, different opinions will be formed. As long as the connection subsists between his reason and his self-love, his opinions and his passions will have a reciprocal influence on each other . . . .
>
> No man is allowed to be a judge in his own cause; because his interest would certainly bias his judgment and, not improbably, corrupt his integrity . . . .
>
> It is in vain to say that enlightened statesmen will be able to adjust . . . clashing interests and render them all subservient to the public good. Enlightened statesmen will not always be at the helm; nor, in many cases, can such an adjustment be made at all, without taking into view indirect and remote considerations, which will rarely prevail over the immediate interest which one party may find in disregarding the rights of another or the good of the whole . . . .
>
> If the impulse and the opportunity be suffered to coincide, we well know that neither moral nor religious motives can be relied on as an adequate control.

These principles have been applied to the governance of schools by the Supreme Court in its most basic statement about public school students' rights:

> The Fourteenth Amendment, as now applied to the states, protects the citizen against the state itself and all of its creatures—boards of education not excepted. These have, of course, important, delicate, and highly dis-

cretionary functions, but none that they may not perform within the limits of the Bill of Rights. That they are educating the young for citizenship is reason for scrupulous protection of constitutional freedoms of the individual.

Federal judges and other persons steeped in the Madisonian system have increasingly pressed our public schools to adopt that system in place of the traditional one. That is the crux of today's difficulty.

Since for two centuries we have run schools on the Puritan system within a broader society run more or less on Madisonian principles, we may reasonably ask whether it isn't possible for us to continue. I believe it is not. There is no sign that the tide of anti-authoritarianism pressing for change will abate. Even if it should, though, three other considerations suggest that the Puritan system must go.

First, as our governmental structure becomes more and more unified, we can expect that sooner or later our national governance system, where it conflicts with a different one, will prevail.

Second, the kind of social environment provided by the Madisonian system is inescapably much more educational than the kind the Puritan system provides. While the Puritan system conveys to the student that he is a lesser being, not to be trusted, the Madisonian system shows him respect. The former, with its centralized power, may intimidate him; the latter is more likely to develop his courage and self-reliance. The former provides him with a more regimented and standardized experience; the latter exposes him to variety, discontinuity, and stimulation. The former restricts his opportunities to learn how to make decisions; the latter casts him in the role of a decision maker. In short, a student will learn better how to function as a citizen of a Madisonian society if his school has been governed along Madisonian lines. These conclusions cannot be described as absolutely and firmly established educational principles, but they follow inescapably, or nearly so, from present-day psychological knowledge, whether one's taste runs to Jerome Bruner, Erik Erikson, James Coleman, Fritz Redl, or B. F. Skinner.

Third, the Puritan governance system is fast losing its usefulness for regulating student behavior, for it works only to the extent that students come to school with a built-in tendency to defer to the authority of their elders. Essentially, they must accept the premise that adults are right about what is best for them, must feel deeply uncomfortable about behaving differently from the way they are told to behave, and must respond when school officials appeal to their sense of shame or guilt. To put the matter in Freudian terms, they must have a certain type of superego. In more common language, they must be cowed, at least in part. This is the way most American young people of the past used to be, and it provided the underlying basis for keeping order in school, as anyone over 30 knows.

Cowing a young person, however, is a process that takes persistent pressure over the early years of his life. Hence it can be achieved only by his family,not by the school. But today, for better or for worse, fewer and fewer families are cowing their children.

The other day a 16-year-old student shook his finger in the face of a teacher of my acquaintance. When she said to him, "Don't you shake your finger at me like that," he retorted, "It's my finger, and I have a right to shake it if I want!" Such a degree of self-assertiveness (or arrogance) was rare just a few years ago. Few of us would have dared to talk that way to a teacher or would have had classmates who dared to. Yet nowadays that kind of thing happens constantly. And it is usually the students most likely to get into trouble, those whose behavior the school most wants to regulate, who are the least cowed.

School officials, then, can no longer count on regulating the behavior of obstreperous kids by intimidating them. As superintendent John Letson of Atlanta said recently, "If the students and authorities are on separate sides, look out! The authorities will lose every time." A sad but no longer rare spectacle is the school principal who used to keep order with reprimands, threats, and punishments, but who finds them ineffectual today and becomes frustrated and angry.

That's not the whole story, however. Students who aren't cowed and are nonetheless subjected to threats and punishments tend *just because they aren't cowed* to respond to what they view as attacks on them with hostility and aggression: The very actions intended to improve their behavior make it worse. Even when cracking down brings these students into immediate compliance, it produces more trouble in the long run. Superintendent Robert Findley of Glen Cove, New York, says the "stupidity of the high school situation," especially rigid rules like "having to have a pass to go to the toilet," are the major cause of high school riots. And, remember, no amount of cracking down by itself will bring these young people around. For the growing number of students who come to school self-assertive, then, the Puritan governance system is doomed to be not only ineffective but counter-productive.

Both the fact that the Puritan system is educationally inferior and the fact that it is no longer very effective for keeping order have legal overtones.

Because the law requires that the school educate students properly, students have a legal claim to be dealt with educationally. In principle, then, a school official who attempts to maintain order with rules or practices which are countereducational, or are less educational than they might be, is not discharging his legal obligation. This is not to predict that if students sue on this ground alone they will win in court. It is to say that such lawsuits may well be brought and that they might be won. I know of two haircut cases which were argued in federal court partly on the basis that the regulations constituted affirmative educational malpractice. The concept of actionable educational malpractice is strange and new, but antipoverty lawyers have a tendency to bring suits on just such strange, new bases.

School officials are also required by law to regulate certain aspects of students' conduct and to do so effectively. Professor Goldstein of the University of Pennsylvania calls this one of the school's "host" obligations. In a situation where traditional Puritan governance approaches are ineffective, and where there is no reason to expect them to be otherwise, a school official who relies on them alone and hence fails to keep order is plainly derelict in his duty. He is all the more vulnerable in the face of abundant recent studies concerning new involvement approaches and "behavior modification" techniques that can be very effective indeed. The ineffective practices associated with the Puritan governance system may not be upset in the courts very soon, but they might.

The way out of the dilemma is fairly clear, I believe, but far from easy. Simply replacing the Puritan system with the Madisonian system will not do, of course. School systems are not democracies—Madison would have said "republics"—but are agencies created by the citizenry at large and accountable to it, while partly accountable, too, to the students they are intended to serve. The school's governance system can be a *modified* Madisonian system, however, with many rights and powers guaranteed to students, yet with some powers reserved to school officials, the representatives and employees of the public. The actual division of power between school officials and students should vary, it seems, depending on the students' ages, so as to allow for the range from the very young to 17-year-old adults on the verge of full citizenship. As little children grow older, the governance system should radically expand their rights and prerogatives and radically decrease—nearly to the vanishing point—the restrictions and requirements unilaterally imposed on them, just as many families broaden the prerogatives of their growing children and adolescents year by year, likewise cutting back on autocratic restrictions. Cutting back on school-imposed restrictions does not mean that students necessarily become freer. It means, more likely, that as they grow up more and more of the restrictions on their freedom are restrictions they have accepted by their own choice.

About prerogatives it should be pointed out that having real prerogatives is much more than being involved in decision making in only an advisory capacity. Valuable though such involvement may be, it does not take the place of having the latitude to make final decisions, and thus to make one's own mistakes and achieve one's own successes.

Unfortunately, however, today's school law not only makes no provision for giving students power or prerogatives but implicitly prohibits it. As one liability case after another reveals, it often prevents the school from allowing students to play on a playground or hang around together after lunch without a supervisor standing by to intervene should any roughness threaten. Recently the California Supreme Court, in a decision involving a high school senior, said:

Supervision during recess and lunch periods is required, in part, so that discipline may be maintained and student conduct regulated . . . . Adolescent high school students are not adults and should not be expected to exhibit that degree of discretion, judgment, and concern for the safety of themselves and others which we associate with full maturity . . . . Boys of 17 and 18 years of age . . .are not accustomed to exercise the same amount of care for their own safety as persons of more mature years . . . . [A] principal task of supervisors is to anticipate and curb rash student behavior. *(Dailey* v. *Los Angeles Unified School District,* 1970)

Such a view seems somewhat anomalous in a state where a year later one of the houses of the state legislature was to vote to define 18-year-olds as in every sense full-fledged adults, but it reflects a general legal barrier to converting the schools to the Madisonian system. As attorney Thomas A. Shannon of the San Diego school district told a Senate committee on education in Sacramento, the law today works on a double standard. This being so, it seems clear that new statutory provisions are needed to allow school officials to turn over to students, especially older ones, significant portions of the regulation of their own conduct and of the general decision making about school affairs, including student publications and the expenditure of certain funds.

It is another key feature of the Madisonian system that rights and duties are recorded in writing. Many school systems have written statements specifying students' duties vis-a-vis the school, and some now have statements of students' rights, though none that I know of ties duties or rights to age, and few even begin to place them on ascending or descending scales. The same holds for the several state board documents spelling out students' rights. Only one document, to my knowledge, affirmatively and explicitly spells out school officials' duties toward students.

During the interim, while new disciplinary approaches are being introduced and new legal instruments created, our school administrators are hardly to be envied. Others, however, can help. Members of the public, especially parents, can press school administrators and school boards to adopt and implement statements of students' rights. New York, Philadelphia, Rochester, Montgomery County (Maryland), Cleveland, Evanston, Minneapolis, Seattle, and many other school systems have already done this; the Ohio state school board and the California state legislature are considering doing it for all public schools in their respective states. Those who know teachers and students can stir them up to insist upon a new distribution of authority and power in the schools and support them when they do. Professors of law and education in particular may be prevailed upon to turn their attention and that of their students to the creation of new legal and educational forms consistent with the Madisonian system.

With plenty of help—including some strong pressure—and with a bit of good luck, administrators will probably be able to extricate themselves from their dilemma, to the profit of us all, but especially of the students in our schools.

Punishment

Is It Time To Stop Beating Schoolchildren?

The American School Board Journal

Corporal punishment doesn't work. Forget the bleeding hearts who whine that it's a humiliating experience, forget the rubes who bluster that it builds character. Corporal punishment simply doesn't work. That, certainly, is the message from psychologists, researchers and some longtime physical punishment practitioners who have taken a close look and a new look at corporal punishment. Their message, like the one Joshua blared in front of the walls of Jericho, may crumble the argument in favor of corporal punishment in the schools.

You need convincing. Try this: If corporal punishment effectively controls behavior, why does it have to be used over and over? Why do the same children need to be paddled and switched again and again? Says one school official: "I've never known anybody to improve his behavior by being beat up . . . . It is only in the very, very extreme cases that punishment is needed, and the school shouldn't have to deal with those cases. When a child's behavior is so extreme and it disrupts the school, he should be referred to his parents or even to the police."[1]

There's more, this time in form of a psychological report: "Through reward, behavior may be stamped in; but the converse—that through punishment it can be stamped out—does not hold. Whereas reinforcement can be controlled to good advantage, in the long run punishment works to the disadvantage of both the punished organism and the punishing agency. Its results are neither predictable nor dependable. Extinction—permitting a behavior to die out by not reinforcing it—and not punishment is the appropriate response for breaking habits."[2]

These psychologists and teachers are telling us that a tennis shoe across the posterior of a child who's late for gym class probably won't

---

[1]Felton, John. "Corporal Punishment: To Paddle or Not To . . . It's Still an Issue." *Dayton Journal Herald*, January 3, 1972.

[2]Bigge, Morris L., and Hunt, Maurice P. *Psychological Foundations of Education.* Harper's Series on Teaching, Harper & Bros., New York, 1962.

help that child become punctual. A crack on the wrist of a classroom giggler won't establish that child's in-class sobriety. Corporal punishment doesn't work.

Does it hurt?

Yes: "Psychologists are unanimously agreed that corporal punishment is a totally ineffective disciplinary device. In fact, there is strong evidence that the results produced by it are the *opposite* of the results desired. Instead of making children more cooperative and compliant with school regulations, corporal punishment is likely to increase both their hostility towards school authority and the behavioral problems which, in part, reflect this hostility."[3]

Yes: "The general public, ignorant of the fact that the history of the typical delinquent reveals frequent and severe corporal punishment, is convinced that all that is needed to curb delinquency is a return to the woodshed type of discipline in home and school."[4]

Yes: " . . . the practice [of corporal punishment] is unavoidably subject to serious abuse by teachers and principals alike; and adults administering violent punishment provide . . .models of violence, and perhaps also of the discarding of inhibitions against indulging in physical aggression, which undoubtedly contributes to violent tendencies in later life."[5]

Corporal punishment doesn't help much with behavioral problems and may harm some children, but still it is needed to protect teachers.

Sorry, but that paddle argument has splinters, too. The National Education Association, which represents *teachers*, has issued a task force report that recommends "all educators move immediately to phase out, over a one-year period . . .infliction of physical pain upon students, except for the purposes of restraint or protection of self or other students."

Teachers who break the corporal punishment habit aren't exactly putting themselves in any additional mortal danger. Most corporal punishment is aimed at tots who do not pose a physical threat to teachers, while student bruisers seldom are recipients of swats. A survey found that many districts restrict the use of corporal punishment to K-6 teachers and "almost all say the practice of corporal punishment does not apply to secondary schools."

One principal admitted that he was hitting smaller children harder than bigger children and realized that he "had better stop hitting any kids."

A parent said he understood that "teachers need to maintain orderly classrooms and, sometimes, even have to protect themselves from unruly students. After all, I spank my kids when they need it. But one male teacher in our area grabbed a little girl by the hair, hit her head on

[3]Waxman, Henry A. (California legislature) in a letter to the president of the Los Angeles school board. January, 1972.

[4]Cutts, Norma A., and Moseley, Nicholas. *Teaching the Disorderly Pupil in Elementary and Secondary School.* Longmans, Green and Co., New York, 1957.

[5]Reithman, Follman and Ladd. "Corporal Punishment in the Public Schools." American Civil Liberties Union, New York, 1972.

her desk, and then slapped her—all because she was talking in class. I'd never do that to one of my children, and a school teacher better not do it to one of my kids, either."

Based on testimony and research, the N.E.A. task force on corporal punishment offered these 16 conclusions:

"1. Physical punishment is an inefficient way to maintain order; it usually has to be repeated over and over.

"2. Physical punishment may increase disruptive behavior.

"3. Physical punishment hinders learning.

"4. Physical punishment is not suitable for any children, regardless of their socioeconomic status.

"5. Physical punishment is most often used on students who are physically weaker and smaller than the teacher.

"6. Physical punishment is often a symptom of frustration rather than a disciplinary procedure.

"7. Infliction of physical punishment is detrimental to the professional educator.

"8. Physical punishment does not develop self-discipline.

"9. Physical punishment develops aggressive hostility.

"10. Physical punishment teaches that might is right.

"11. Physical punishment by educators is not comparable to that in-flicted by parents.

"12. Students may prefer physical punishment to other alternatives offered them.

"13. Limitations on the way physical punishment is to be used are often regularly ignored.

"14. Physical punishment is legal in many places, but its constitutionality is being challenged in several court suits.

"15. The availability of physical punishment discourages teachers from seeking more effective means of discipline.

"16. The use of physical punishment inclines everyone in the school community to regard students as less than human and the school as dehumanizing."[6]

After reviewing the evidence against the use of corporal punishment, some officials still might sigh: "Yeah, corporal punishment is an unpleasant tool, but it's the only one we have."

That simply is not true. Many nonphysical methods of controlling student behavior are available and are being used. The American Civil Liberties Union considers the "corporal-punishment-is-all-we-have" argument to be a rotten one:

"[Another] justification given for keeping corporal punishment . . .is that we can't get rid of it until we have provided alternatives. What is tragically lacking here is the insight that so long as there is institutionalizing of corporal punishment, with its use sanctioned by higher authority, it will be a barrier to the development of other alternatives . . . .

---

[6]The "Report of the Task Force On Corporal Punishment" was published by the National Education Association, Washington, D.C., 1972.

"The continuance of the practice is urged [by proponents] because abolishment . . . would be too fundamental a change, which could not be achieved without staff development and extensive retraining. What a shocking comment—that complete re-education of our educators would be necessary in order to run the schools without hitting children."[7]

The legal indictment against corporal punishment, if there is one, is based on the fact that agents of the *state* (public school officials) are administering the punishment. The legal question: Does the state have the right to use physical punishment against children?

When corporal punishment cases do reach court, school officials usually have been given their head and their hand in dealing with student discipline. Judges generally have not interfered unless school officials have acted in an arbitrary, capricious or unreasonable manner. (Next month in the JOURNAL, C. A. Hollister will explain what the courts have said about school discipline and will unravel the trends in current school discipline litigation and legal rulings.)

In the *Cooper v. McJunkin* case, decided 120 years ago, Indiana Supreme Court Judge Stuart commented:

"The husband can no longer moderately chastise his wife; nor, according to the more recent authorities, the master his servant or apprentice. Even the degrading cruelties of the naval service have been arrested. Why the person of the schoolboy, 'with his shining morning face,' should be less sacred in the eye of the law than that of the apprentice or the sailor, is not easily explained."

In some American cities, school officials are not allowed to slap the "shining morning faces" of schoolboys and schoolgirls. Corporal punishment *is* banned in London (once famous or infamous for caning) and in France, and, yes, in the Soviet Union.

For school officials who—after examining the evidence—still insist that misbehaving school children be beaten, here's a sort of a slap-in-the-face message: Better check your own psyche for hidden hangups.

Reithman, Follman and Ladd, *loc cit.*

The Case Against Short Suspensions

Patricia M. Lines

Staff Attorney, Harvard Center for Law and Education

A good citizen of a town has seen a girl on the way to school sipping from what appears to be a whiskey bottle. In a fit of civic duty, he reaches for the telephone: when the girl arrives at school (cold sober), she is sent home at once for—eight days. In a hamlet 50 miles away a teacher sees a girl smoking in the lavatory, or perhaps she smelled smoke and concluded that where there's smoke . . . . The teacher reports it to the principal—who sends the girl home for three days. Seventy-five miles to the north, a boy sleepily crawls into his Levi's and heads for school. When he arrives, he walks past a school counselor who sends him home. In a central city a black kid is suspended for disturbing the class and fighting. Three whites were also involved, but they are not punished. Meanwhile, back at the hamlet, a boy is suspended for the fourth time for "insubordination"—for distributing his underground newsletter, which school officials find distasteful. (The paper finds school officials distasteful.) He is suspended for seven days—and has been suspended for a total of 16 days throughout the year.

In each of these situations, the student's suspension was for a short period of time—one half to eight days. In each, the students were summarily deprived of their right to attend school. They were not allowed even two minutes to protest their innocence before an impartial person.

These cases are typical. Lawyers at the Center for Law and Education have been besieged recently with requests to help students who have been suspended for a relatively small number of days without any kind of hearing. Short-term suspensions seem to enjoy considerable popularity among school officials, for it gives them an easy way out when faced with a disciplinary problem. A school official does not have to take the time for a hearing required for longer suspensions

Inequality in Education, July 1972. Reprinted with permission of the Center for Law and Education, Harvard University.

(and incidentally, does not have to run the risk of being vetoed by another school official—the hearing officer). Short-term suspension is also faster and less troublesome than detention, which requires supervision by school personnel, or counseling, which requires specially trained personnel. Whatever the reasons for its widespread use, the short-term suspension practice presents itself as a serious constitutional problem.

Short-term suspensions allow school officials—usually principals—to make on-the-spot decisions which may often be wrong. These suspensions sometimes represent punishment for constitutionally protected activity—such as the distribution of a newsletter. Suspension patterns at any given school may also discriminate unfairly against poor or minority students who are disciplined more stringently than others. Some situations involve "offenses" which are at least marginally protected by the Constitution, or are so trivial that punishment by suspension is excessive—wearing blue jeans, for example, or smoking. Other offenses clearly warrant some disciplinary action, if the charges are true, but the punishment is far too severe. In any case, the culpability of the student should not be relevant to the question of due process. Ironically, the student's chances of winning a favorable court decision often depend on whether the judge believes him guilty of the charges underlying the suspension. The real issue in all these cases, however, is the legality of a punishment which denies students a precious and valuable right—the right to attend school—without first granting them a hearing where they can contest the charges against them. This article argues that the length of the suspension should not, in any way, affect the student's right to procedural due process.

The Right to Education

Short-term suspensions are a denial of a very important and precious right—the right to schooling—which has been affirmed repeatedly by the courts. The most frequently quoted passage on this point is found in *Brown v. Board of Education*, where Chief Justice Warren wrote:

> Today, education is perhaps the most important function of state and local governments. Compulsory school attendance laws and the great expenditures for education both demonstrate our recognition of the importance of education to our democratic society. It is required in the performance of our most basic public responsibilities, even service in the armed forces. It is the very foundation of good citizenship. Today it is a principal instrument in awakening the child to cultural values, in preparing him for later professional training, and in helping him to adjust normally to his environment. In these days, it is doubtful that any child may reasonably be expected to succeed in life if he is denied the opportunity of an education . . . .347 U.S. 483,493 (1954).

This precept has been adopted wholeheartedly in lower courts. The *Brown* language was adopted by the Fifth Circuit for example, in a student due process case, *Williams v. Dade County School Board*, where the court also held that:

> it requires no argument to demonstrate that education is vital and, indeed, basic to civilized society. Without sufficient education the plaintiffs would not be able to earn an adequate livelihood, to enjoy life to the fullest, or to fulfill as completely as possible the duties and responsibilities of good citizens. 441 F.2d 299, 302 (5th Cir. 1971).

It was again cited in *Hosier v. Evans*, a case involving access to education, where the federal district court for the Virgin Islands, found public education "so fundamental as to be fittingly considered the cornerstone of a vibrant and viable republican form of democracy" [302 F. Supp. 316, 319 (D.St. Croix 1970]. Likewise, in *Ordway v. Hargraves* [323 F. Supp. 1155, 1158 (D.-Mass. 1971)], the federal district court in Massachusetts noted that "It would seem beyond argument that the right to receive a public school education is a basic personal right," and refused to allow the exclusion from school of a healthy pregnant girl. In *Chandler v. South Bend Community School Corporation* an Indiana district court found education "a substantial right implicit in the 'liberty' assurance of the Due Process Clause," and a necessary element in the effective exercise of rights guaranteed by the first eight amendments to the U.S. Constitution [Civ. No. 71-S-51 (N.D. Ind. Aug. 26, 1971)].

In *Sullivan v. Houston Independent School District*, a federal district court in Texas, Judge Seals, ruled:

> Education . . . is a priceless commodity. Furthermore, it is a fundamental right of every citizen. Just as the Supreme Court has declared that United States citizenship cannot be revoked except by voluntary expatriation . . . so courts should declare that an individual's guarantee of an education, only quantitatively less basic than the right of citizenship, cannot be annulled, even temporarily, except in the most extreme circumstances. 333 F. Supp. 1149, 1172 (S.D. Tex. 1971).

There can be no question that education is a vitally important right, resting in part on express state constitutional provisions, and, in part, on the essential contribution of education to the effective exercise of the entire Bill of Rights.

Temporary Suspension of a Right

Although virtually all courts recognize a valuable and important right to education, most have allowed summary short-term suspensions of this right. Courts have consistently held that a hearing is required prior to expulsion from school, or a suspension for a "substantial" period of time, but have allowed shorter suspensions without a hearing. This distinction is difficult to justify. Its very arbitrariness has fostered wide disagreement in the federal judiciary over what is "substantial." The standard, of necessity, has to be measured in terms of numbers of days out of school, and courts have variously held that students may be excluded from school without a hearing for from three to 15 days.[1] This kind of analysis is faulty, for if a right to education exists, it exists every day a young person is entitled to go to school. The court's analysis is like holding that procedural safeguards do not have to be followed if a state agency takes one or two percent of a man's land, rather than 10 or 100 percent.

Temporary Suspension of a Privilege

Even if education were deemed a mere privilege and of no constitutional significance, the temporary suspension of the enjoyment of a privilege must, under certain circumstances, be preceded by a hearing. The hearing requirement depends on the likelihood of injury. Thus, the Supreme Court has required hearings prior to the temporary suspension of welfare and wage payments, and a driver's license. In Goldberg v. Kelly [397 U.S. 254 (1970)], the Court held that a welfare cut-off must be preceded by a hearing. In Sniadach v. Family Finance Corporation [395 U.S. 337 (1969)], it struck down an ex parte garnishment. In Bell v. Burson [91 S.Ct. 1586 (1971)], it invalidated a prehearing suspension of a driver's and car licenses. Allowing summary suspensions from school for short periods of time is like allowing a welfare cut-off or a garnishment or a license suspension three (or 20) days before a hearing. The language in Goldberg, Sniadach, and Bell left no room for such concessions, and courts should not do so in school cases.[2]

Moreover, suspensions from school can be vastly more damaging than the temporary suspension of welfare or wage payments. The welfare recipient in Goldberg could have claimed payments retroactively at the hearing which was scheduled to take place after the cut-off. The employee in Sniadach, faced with a garnishment order freezing only $31.59 in wages, could expect to enjoy the free use of this money after prevailing at trial. Yet, the court ordered a prior hearing in both cases. A more serious loss faces the suspended student. There is no such thing as a temporary postponement of schooling. Suspension inevitably involves a permanent denial of access to education for the days missed; they cannot be recouped.

Injury to the Student

Whether attendance at school is a right or a privilege, temporary suspension can do serious injury to the student, interfering with his education in a variety of ways. (S)he can slip behind in school work and never fully catch up with the rest of the class. A particularly valuable and interesting area of study may be opened and closed while (s)he is

---

[1] Sullivan v. Houston Indep. School Dist., 307 F. Supp. 528 (S.D. Tex. 1969), 333 F. Supp. 1149 (S.D. Tex. 1971) (3 days); Black Students of North Fort Meyers Jr.-Sr. High School ex. rel. Shoemaker v. Williams, 317 F. Supp. 1211 (M.D. Fla. 1970) (less than 10 days); Williams v. Dade County School Board, 441 F.2d 229 (5th Cir. 1971) (10 days, insubstantial; 40 days, substantial); Baker v. Downey City Board of Education, 307 F. Supp. 517 (C.D. Cal. 1969) (10 days); Farrell v. Joel, 437 F.2d 160 (2d Cir. 1971) (10 or 15 days or more).

[2] It is still an open question whether a hearing is required before a partial cutoff in funds, before a reduction takes place in welfare payments. Daniel v. Goliday, 398 U.S. 73 (1970) (remanding to district court for determination of injury due to reduction).

excluded from school. Worse, if the student is already having trouble in school, the suspension might be the "straw that broke the camel's back"—(s)he might become so discouraged that a short-term suspension will ultimately lead him or her to "drop out." As Judge Seals observed on deciding the second *Sullivan* case, "The student may choose not to return at all. Without encouragement from school and family to continue his education, he may view himself as a failure, and his fate as deserved" [333 F. Supp. at 1172].

Stigma and Due Process

There is yet another, independent ground for requiring a hearing prior to suspension. Regardless of the student's right to schooling, government officials may not summarily stigmatize individuals without a hearing. The Supreme Court in *Wisconsin v. Constantineau* found unconstitutional a state statute which allowed law enforcement officers to post notices in liquor stores and bars instructing the proprietors not to sell liquor to persons they believed alcoholic. The court noted that before attaching this "label" to an individual—which was to some, but not all, people "a stigma or badge of disgrace"—procedural due process had to be followed, and a full adversary hearing held [400 U.S. 436 (1971)].

School suspensions also represent a "badge of disgrace" to many people. A suspension represents a decision by school authorities that a particular student is a problem child, undesirable, or, as Judge Seals stated in *Sullivan II*, an "outcast."[3] He observed:

> In addition, suspension is a particularly humiliating punishment evoking images of the public penitent of medieval Christendom and colonial Massachusetts, the outlaw of the American West, and the ostracized citizen of classical Athens. Suspension is an officially-sanctioned judgment that a student be for some period removed beyond the pale. 333 F. Supp. at 1172.

Legal Precedent

The proper view then, is to require a hearing for any suspension, regardless of length. This position, while novel in most jurisdictions, has been affirmed by a few federal district courts. In a Massachusetts case a judge preliminarily enjoined a school committee from excluding students from school without a hearing [*Mello v. School Committee of New Bedford*, C.A. No. 72-1146-F (D.Mass. Ap. 6, 1972) Clearinghouse Number 7773]. He set no time limits or exceptions in the order, which specifically required prior notice, right to counsel, right to present evidence and question adverse witnesses, and a right to a decision in writing based exclusively on evidence adduced at the hearing. Likewise, in a Wisconsin case the court ruled that "Unless the element

---

[3]333F. Supp. at 1172. See also, *Kahl v. Breen*, 296 F. Supp. 702, 707 (W.D. Wis. 1969), *affirmed*, 419 F.2d 1034 (7th Cir. 1969), *cert. denied*, 398 U.S. 937 (1970).

of danger to persons or property is present, suspension should not occur without specification of charges, notice of hearing, and hearing."[4] In a Kansas case, a judge ordered a college student returned to his campus, after he had been suspended without a hearing for carrying a firearm on campus. About seven weeks after the suspension, the judge heard the case and immediately ordered officials to take the student back until a hearing was held. He observed that summary suspension would be appropriate in emergency situations, but three weeks was too long even for an emergency suspension [*Gardenhire v. Chalmers*, 326 F. Supp. 1200, 1205, (D. Kan. 1971)].

These decisions, although representing a minority view, are in harmony with the Supreme Court decisions requiring prior hearings in welfare, garnishment and license suspension cases. They represent a more reasoned view than the bulk of the cases, which allow arbitrary decisions affecting a student's right to schooling, so long as the decision contains appropriate time limitations.

The Interests of School Officials

Constitutional rights may be suspended under limited circumstances where the interests of the state are sufficiently compelling to warrant such an unusual action. These circumstances do not exist in the run-of-the-mill school suspension situation, for there is no justification for avoiding a hearing prior to a short-term suspension. The cost to the school is the price of a postage stamp (notice) and a few man-hours of time (hearing). All that is asked is that school authorities take steps to assure that the charges underlying the disciplinary action are true, and the action appropriate. They are asked only to notify the student, hear him, allow him to confront adverse witnesses, and to rest discipline on an impassioned and reasoned decision, based on the hearing. If the student is culpable, this will postpone punishment until the hearing is held, but it is entirely likely that the discipline will be as effective. In many cases, summary suspensions also take place after the act, as when principals suspend students on hear-say evidence that they were smoking. The timing of the suspension has no special importance.

The cost of a hearing is small; the value of on-the-spot suspension is negligible. In addition, the existence and conduct of the hearing can be an educational process in itself, contributing to the ultimate goal of order in the school. A student is much more likely to respect school rules and the school disciplinary process if they appear rational and fair to him. In contrast, students who are suspended on-the-spot by a principal generally view the principal as authoritarian and hostile, and their attitude toward school officialdom becomes rebellious.

---

[4]*Stricklin v. Regents*, 297 F. Supp. 416, 420 (W.D. Wis. 1969). The court went on to say:

The preliminaries to the hearing and the hearing itself should constitute what I have called a "full hearing"; that is, a procedure which affords all of the elements of due process which must constitutionally precede the imposition of the sanction of expulsion or the imposition of the sanction of suspension for a substantial period of time. The last phrase might be construed to allow for summary suspensions, but this would clearly negate the passage in the text. The entire sentence defines the phrase "full hearing" and it is clear the judge was extending the hearing requirements for long-term suspensions to short-term situations.

Emergency Suspension

Occasions exist when removal from classes, or from the school, may be an appropriate measure for dealing with an emergency situation— to restore order in a school which has been seriously disrupted or to remove a clearly dangerous student. School officials have an obligation to avoid a clear and present danger to the school, students and teachers, and to prevent serious and prolonged disruptions of the educational process. The rule against pre-hearing *punitive* suspensions does not preclude emergency action, but it does preclude any suspension that lasts beyond the minimum time necessary to restore order. An emergency suspension which lasts beyond a minimal "cooling off period" should be treated as a disciplinary reprisal by school authorities, and should be preceded by notice and hearing.

The permissible length of the emergency suspension depends on the circumstances. Where a small number of students are engaged in a ruckus, the adults in charge could reasonably expect that the kids would be calm and orderly by the next day, and suspension should last only until the end of the current school day. Students exhibiting more violent propensities might warrant suspension until hearings could be held. In the Kansas case, for example, the student reportedly carried a firearm to school and had been criminally charged with attempted murder—clearly a cause for alarm, if true. The judge observed that five to fifteen days would be a reasonable period of time for a temporary or interim emergency suspension, but he found the period from December 10 (the date of suspension) to February 1 (the date of his decision) too long [*Gardenhire v. Chalmers*, 326 F. Supp. 1200, 1205 (D. Kan. 1971)]. The alleged danger was not diminished, but the judge apparently felt that school authorities in this situation should have and could have arranged for a hearing before February 1. If it can be shown that a hearing could be held within five days, for example, courts should not allow emergency suspensions of more than five days, even in the case of a clearly violent student. The extent of presumed guilt of the person to be suspended for emergency reasons provides no excuse for failure to observe due process.

Signs of Judicial Doubt

Courts holding the majority view—that summary short-term suspensions are appropriate—have had some difficulty in coming to grips with their own rule. The Second Circuit, for example, allowed a ten-day suspension of a girl involved in an administration office sit-in. It forgot the time honored precept that a man is innocent until proven guilty, and found that the girl's actions were "clearly improper" [*Farrell v. Joel*, 437 F.2d 160, 163 (1971)]. The court uneasily observed that there might be cases where such clarity does not exist. The court suggested that the school promulgate "fair and reasonable" procedures for suspensions in order to "give those affected a fair opportunity to question whether an alleged violation of a school rule actually occurred and what penalty, if any, would be appropriate" [437

F.2d at 163- 64]. The court fails to suggest how the threshold decision of "clearly improper" is to be made, however. Possibly it was swayed by the emergency situation revealed in the facts of the case, and was unaware of the widespread use of summary suspensions for trivial matters.

A bad factual situation seems to have influenced at least one other court—a Florida district court. In deciding that school officials must have authority to summarily suspend students, the court constructed a number of hypothetical examples, all of which required an immediate suspension. Thus, the court reasoned, a hearing would require the absence of teachers and pupils from class, and in general disrupt the normal school day [Banks v. Board of Public Instruction, 314 F.Supp. 285 (S.D. Fla. 1970)]. The emergency rule above should be sufficient to allow summary treatment of truly emergency situations. The Fifth Circuit, in noting this decision, interpreted it as a means of giving school officials an "administrative device utilized to remove unruly students at a particularly tense time" [Williams v. Dade County School Board, 441 F.2d 299, 301 (1971)]. Such a rule is not justified when applied to students who are suspended for offenses which are over and done with by the time school officials hear of them. A girl who is suspended for tippling on the way to school is not disrupting activities at the school; there is no need for an immediate suspension or to exclude her from school the moment the offense is reported. In fact, the school would probably operate more smoothly if such reports were taken and processed with a modicum of due process.

Preliminary Hearings

Even if courts continue to regard one to 15 days out of school as "insubstantial," it does not necessarily follow that hearings should be waived. The decision to waive hearing requirements reflects a decision that the state's interest outweighs the student's in such circumstances. The balance could be tipped in favor of the student by simplifying the hearing requirements. In other words, courts could abbreviate rather than cancel the hearing requirement. Short-term suspensions (e.g., up to three days) might take place after an impartial school official has questioned the student and the complaining party in the student's presence and has made a finding that the student did in fact violate a school rule, and that a lesser discipline (such as detention) is not sufficient. Such a hearing, abbreviated in this way, need only take a few minutes. Yet it discourages "on the spot" suspensions by officials who may not be impartial and who may even be the complaining party.

This approach was adopted for emergency suspensions in the Wisconsin and Kansas cases discussed above. In Stricklin v. Board of Regents the court had held that a disciplinary suspension requires a prior hearing, and then went on to note:

> When the appropriate university authority has reasonable cause to believe that danger will be present if a student is permitted to remain on

the campus pending a decision following a full hearing, an interim suspension may be imposed. But the question persists whether such an interim suspension may be imposed without a prior "preliminary hearing" of any kind. The constitutional answer is inescapable. An interim suspension may not be imposed without a prior preliminary hearing, unless it can be shown that it is impossible or unreasonably difficult to accord it prior to an interim suspension, procedural due process requires that he be provided such a preliminary hearing at the earliest practical time.

*   *   *   *

In this opinion I have used the term "preliminary hearing" to denote procedures less rigorous than those (referred to as a "full hearing") which must precede the ultimate imposition of a serious disciplinary sanction. I have not undertaken to define the ingredients of a minimally adequate "preliminary hearing" . . . . 297 F.Supp. 416, 420, 422 (D. Wis. 1969).

Courts which have held that school officials may suspend students for three to 15 days without a hearing should have at least required an abbreviated hearing.

Elements of a Preliminary Hearing

The same judge—Judge Doyle—subsequently heard a case involving a clear emergency situation. A group of students, some of whom actually fired weapons, invaded a fraternity house, doing considerable damage to persons and property [*Buck v. Carter*, 308 F. Supp. 1246 (W.D. Wis. 1970)]. Following the requirements of *Stricklin*, school officials called in the students for a prior preliminary hearing.

At this preliminary hearing, officials took no action against two students who specifically denied being present at the raid and suspended the remainder pending a full hearing which was to take place in three weeks. (The timing did not require many days of absence from school because of Christmas and New Year's vacations.) The officials found the temporary action warranted because the students' "continued presence on this campus poses a clear and present danger to the university community" and the students themselves. The students sought relief from Judge Doyle, who found that the officials must take the following steps in a preliminary hearing (*id.* at 1248-49):

1. Make an "initial evaluation of the reliability of the information received . . ." as to both the incident and the individuals involved.

2. Determine that the conduct was such as "reasonably to indicate that the prompt separation" of the student is warranted for reasons relating to the safety and well being of persons and property.

3. Allow the student "at the earliest opportunity" to appear before a school official, be notified of the charges against him, and to make a statement.

   The court noted that if the student admits guilt, the officials may end the hearing there, but if the student offers a plausible denial, they should investigate further.

Judge Doyle found that these steps were taken, with a possible exception that notice was deficient. He denied relief, however, since the students had given cautious and limited responses without specifically denying being present at the raid.

Time Limits

If short-term suspensions are allowed, despite this analysis, courts must decide the initial question—how long should they be? At what point does the time out of school become "substantial"? Unlike emergency suspensions where the length of exclusion is governed largely by an assessment of the present danger to people and property in the school, summary disciplinary suspensions have no rational basis and require an arbitrary time cut-off. Recognizing that the cut-off is arbitrary, courts should make it as small as possible—one or two days. Among courts holding the majority view and allowing summary suspension, the best view was articulated in *Sullivan v. Houston Independent School District*. In 1969, Judge Seals ordered substantial revisions of the procedures to be followed prior to disciplinary suspension in Houston schools [*Sullivan* II, 307 F. Supp. 1328 (S.D. Tex.)]. The court's order exempted suspensions "specifically limited to three days at the time of imposition." On reopening the case at the request of a second student (Paul Kitchen) who was suspended in circumstances very similar to the original Sullivan suspensions, the court continued to permit three-day suspensions at the discretion of the principal, urging that its use should be restricted to discipline of "the incorrigible when all other means fail" [*Sullivan* II, 333 F. Supp. 1149, 1174 (S.D. Tex. 1971)]. Other courts have not been as precise in specifying the number of days they would allow in a summary suspension, but a Florida district judge has decided ten days are too many,[5] and the Fifth Circuit has cited this opinion with approval and noted that "we feel that even a ten-day suspension is a serious penalty" [*Williams v. Dade County School Board*, 441 F.2d 299, 301 (1971)].

A three-day rule is manageable. No evidence of difficulty was evidenced in Houston. Judge Seals observed, in fact, that one principal never found it necessary to suspend students without a hearing, except in emergency situations. The three-day rule is also in use in Tyler, Texas, notably only because a federal judge reprinted it in his decision requiring Tyler to adhere to its own rule [*Dunn v. Tyler Independent School District*, 327 F. Supp. 528, 531-32, n.2 (E.D. Tex. 1971)]. Severe limitations have also been adapted in Pittsburgh (semi-voluntarily) where principals may suspend a student for up to three days in an emergency situation (and where the misconduct is witnessed by the principal), or following a principal's investigation. The required in-

---

[5] *Black Students of North Forth Meyers Jr.-Sr. High School ex rel. Shoemaker v. Williams*, 317 F. Supp. 1211 (M.D. Fla. 1970), vacated on other grounds, 443 F.2d 1350 (5th Cir. 1971), redecided, 335 F. Supp. 820 (M.D. Fla. 1972).

vestigation in Pittsburgh is really an abbreviated hearing before the principal.[6]

One final word: where courts allow temporary suspensions without a full hearing, they should also impose a maximum number of days, such as five days total, during which a student may be excluded from school in any school year pursuant to summary procedures, to avoid harsh results where officials repeatedly impose short-term suspensions on the same student. Thus, a student would receive a full hearing on his second or third offense, even if the suspension were only for one day, if he had been excluded from school without a full hearing for five days on previous occasions in the same school year. Anything short of this allows arbitrary decisions which can result in serious injury to a vitally important right—the right to be in school.

Summary

Suspension of a student from school for disciplinary purposes should always be preceded by a hearing. Emergency suspensions (without a hearing) may take place if there is a clear and present danger to persons or property in the school. If judges permit short-term suspensions without a full hearing, they should at least require an abbreviated hearing. And if they permit summary suspensions, they should severely limit their length.

---

[6]A state court has ordered the school district to adopt rules for a "fair and prompt hearing to be afforded to all students suspended from school for disciplinary reasons . . . ." *Travis v. Kunkel*, No. 2507 (Ct. Com. Pleas, Allegheny County, Penn., preliminary injunction, Dec. 18, 1971). Later, parties agreed to a rule allowing principals to suspend students for up to three days on the basis of an abbreviated hearing; and for two days in an emergency situation, plus one additional day, where necessary. Pittsburgh Board of Public Education, Procedures for Dealing with Student Misconduct, March 23, 1971, sec. 4; see also sec. 3, sec. 5. Longer suspensions require more elaborate procedures. The court approved these procedures in a consent order of June, 1971.

Behaviorism

Values Versus Techniques: An Analysis of Behavior Modification

Clifford K. Madsen

Associate Professor of Music
Florida State University, Tallahassee

An answer to some of the criticisms of behavior mod

A teacher stops by a child working on math and checks correct/incorrect responses. This teacher has observed that most students learn more efficiently when they are given academic feedback. She is using a principle of behavior modification to improve academic performance.

The same teacher sees another child engrossed in his work assignment. She moves quickly to his seat, gives him a smile, and whispers in his ear, "I'm so happy to see you working on your assignment." She has noticed that if she can praise him while he does his work, he works much more than when she recognizes him while he is not working. She is again using a principle of behavior modification.

The teacher goes back to her desk to correct more academic assignments. A little boy comes quickly to her desk and asks a question. She ignores him completely and calmly goes about correcting her papers. He stays about 15 seconds and then goes back to his work. The teacher smiles to herself as she checks a chart designed for this particular boy. She has almost extinguished his habit of running to her desk (only once this week; initially he did it 28 times a day and that was *after* she started recording it). The teacher sets her handkerchief on her desk as a reminder to go to this child after he has been in his seat for a few minutes. She hopes that his question was not a really important one, that it can wait two or three minutes.

She goes back to correcting assignments. It is important to her that she finish them by the end of the day. She has discovered that, by randomly picking out a different day of the week for children to take corrected papers home, she can dramatically increase their academic performance. Again, behavior modification.

She takes the time to check on the child who came to her desk—he wanted to know if he could get a book from the library—then returns to her seat. She hears Suzy starting to talk to her neighbor. The teacher immediately gets up, goes to Suzy, and firmly tells her that she should stop visiting until her work is done. The teacher notices that

Suzy appears a little sad. She is a sensitive child, and the teacher has long since discovered that a bit of teacher disapproval will halt her inappropriate behavior. Behavior modification.

The teacher remembers that she used to yell nearly all day long (observers actually counted 146 times during one morning session). In those days she used disapproval about 80% of the time in efforts to modify social behavior, generally with little effect. Although she found that this percentage is about average for most teachers, she wanted to be more positive. At first it was difficult, not "natural." She had to learn behavior modification techniques: the reinforcement of certain academic and social behaviors. Now, when she hears a loud adult voice in an adjoining classroom, she thinks about a discussion of honesty she had with a colleague. Should a teacher be honestly disapproving most of the time because it is a "natural" response? She has learned better.

She stands in front of her class. "Children, I would like you to look at me. Suzy's looking at me. Sam is looking at me. Now David's looking at me. Now everyone is looking at me. That's nice." (Again, behavior modification.) "You may all stop your individual work and visit now until it's time for music." (When the youngsters helped make class rules earlier in the year, they expressed a desire for talk time. Establishing rules with student help has *nothing* to do with behavior modification.)

As the students visit, the teacher thinks about the token system the school counselor is trying to establish in some of the rooms. She has read many reports about "token economy" systems and understands that they represent an effective application of behavioral principles, but she does not choose the technique for her class. She has never liked material rewards for learning (except for herself!) and prefers to use social reinforcers instead. Besides, she cannot imagine how her class could be much better than it is. She really likes it. She knows also that the counselor sometimes uses very strong disapproval as well as a special "time-out room" for some children. The effects of his procedures are also well documented and consistent with behavioral approaches, but she prefers not to use them.

What Is Behavior Modification?

The above paragraphs describe procedures whose efficacy has been documented in behavioral research. In essence, this research shows that behavior is maintained and shaped by its consequences. (Strange, isn't it, that so obvious a truth should be so badly used in practice?) *Behavior* is a common word which is used quite casually in reference to many things. In the literature of behavior modification it refers to *anything* a person does, says, or thinks that can be observed directly or indirectly. Behavior modification theory deals with techniques of changing behavior as well as specific interaction effects. A "well-behaved student" is of course a person who behaves in ways that society (represented in school by the teacher) thinks are appropriate to a given situation.

Some people try to make a case against a behavioral approach by alluding to "attitudes" which are not a part of the process of behavior modification. Actually, these attitudes represent different value systems. *Principles* for teaching (shaping appropriate behaviors) should not be confused with value issues. Many teachers regard the questions of why, what, and who as considerably more important than how. But, after the teacher has decided what is to be learned, why it should be learned, and who is going to learn it, then an effective approach to how it will be taught is vital, or the teacher's efforts as well as the student's will be wasted.

A very simple rationale explains the efficiency of behavioral approaches. *Behavioral change occurs for a reason:* Students work for things that bring them pleasure; they work for approval from people they admire; students change behaviors to satisfy the desires they have been taught to value; they generally avoid behaviors they associate with unpleasantness; and finally, students develop habitual behaviors when those behaviors are often repeated. The behavior modification approach derives from psychological experiments and represents nothing more than simple cause and effect relationships.

The current emphasis on behavior modification, or reinforcement theory (to use an older term), grew from the works of B. F. Skinner. Programmed instruction is the best-known result of his initial work. Other teaching systems, treatments of mental illness, and techniques in clinical psychology are based on Skinner's experiments. Many critics disagree with certain value choices and extensions proposed by Skinner, but this in no way invalidates the empirical relationships in learning established and stated by Skinnerian investigators. Indeed, the entire rationale of behavior modification is that most behavior is *learned.* Behavior thus defined includes emotional responses, attitudes, reading, listening, talking, looking into the mirror, liking a person, wanting to talk out a problem, hitting, being frustrated, sticking with a task, abandoning a task, responding appropriately to the desires of a teacher, not responding to the desires of a teacher, most "good" behavior, most "bad" behavior, disturbing one's neighbors, being "well-behaved," being excited about school work, hating to learn, and so on—and on—and on.

Exactly the same principles may be used to teach good social behavior as are used to teach appropriate academic skills (e.g., providing feedback about correct/incorrect responses). If a teacher wishes students to have a real desire to learn something, the teacher may find it necessary to structure the external environment so students will seek structured rewards for their work tasks. After initial manipulation, the rewards for proper behavior will often come from the reinforcement of the particular task itself, i.e., getting the right answer is often all the structure that is needed. Incidentally, this is precisely what most teachers do when they initially make a "game" out of learning. Students become enthusiastic concerning the game per se, not realizing that its purpose is to stimulate effective work. It is curious that some teachers who try desperately to make work fun also say they reject any "manipulation techniques." The teacher's job is to structure learning experiences. This structuring process involved manipulating the environment (i.e., setting up the correct situation, physical plant, materials, and so on) conducive to effective learning, whether the goal be simple obedience, complex problem solving, or self-discovery. The teacher must structure as wisely as possible, whether the school organization is open, free, pod, modular, or something else. One should know the subparts of any complex task and structure the situation so that each student can have a "rewarding learning experience." Irrespective of our cherished clichés, we actually do practice behavioral manipulation. It appears paradoxical for the teacher to reject manipulation when manipulation is the essence of her task.

Behavior Results from Its Consequences

Behavioral research demonstrates that if work tasks can be 1) geared to the student's own level, 2) presented in logical sequence with 3) appropriate feedback concerning correct/incorrect responses, and 4) rewarded for successively better efforts to reach defined goals, then the student will certainly learn. Exactly the same principles apply to teaching proper social skills.

Critics say, "Yes, but isn't that a cold approach?" Certainly not. While behavior modification is the only branch of applied psychology based on scientific principles verified in the laboratory, it is the nature of the material to be learned that represents important value choices. Actually, because of its consistency and simplicity, behavioral modification effected through contingent reinforcement (approval/disapproval) usually represents a very kind and understandable system to students. The behavioral scientist who observes a school situation can classify almost everything that goes on behaviorally, regardless of how well the teachers involved understand principles of reinforcement. Cause and effect behaviors are always present. For example, some teachers do not realize when they are being sarcastic. "Why don't you just yell louder, Jimmy?" Problems are created when the student is not really sure of the teacher's meaning. Being taken literally is the price one sometimes pays for using sarcasm or irony.

The behavioral clinician can demonstrate how teachers might be more effective in the application of the child's or teacher's own values. Many teachers are surprised to learn how closely they approximate a strict behavioral approach. After being apprised of behavioral principles, many exclaim, "Why that's what I've been doing all the time!"

When learning is defined as a change or modification of behavior, then reinforcement principles constitute a method to promote or expedite this learning. In short, behavioral analysis asks, "How should we go about teaching in the best possible manner to ensure correct association?" Or, more specifically, "How should we go about teaching the student to concentrate, to read, to share, to clean his desk, to be honest, to develop his own values?" If a youngster responds favorably to our presentation, we assume that it functions as a reward for the student. But what if the student does not respond? Then we must restructure the external environment so that the student *does* receive proper motivation.

If at First You Don't Succeed?

If behaviors can be learned, they can also be unlearned or relearned. Sometimes, in our zeal to get through to our students, we make mistakes. Sometimes we make mistakes regardless of zeal. The efficacy of behavioral techniques with *severe* problem behaviors within mental hospitals and institutions for the retarded and handicapped perhaps should give us the encouragement to move forward. Behavioral techniques have demonstrated that even severely handicapped children can learn much faster and much more than we previously believed possible. And no, one does not need to be a medical or psychological specialist to provide academic and social approval. Teachers have been doing this for years.

What are the dynamics of changing social behavior? Since it is impossible for a person to maintain two contradictory responses, the skillful teacher will program to elicit responses *incompatible* with deviant behavior and thereby obviate the need for punishment. "Count to 10 before you get angry; think before you begin your work; take three big breaths before you cry." Punishment alone may stop deviant behavior, but it will not necessarily teach correct associations. The child who is hit with his spoon because he cannot use it properly will not necessarily learn proper etiquette. Similarly, the child who is punished for faulty reading will not necessarily learn to read efficiently. The one child might shun the spoon; the other child may stop reading. Setting up incompatible responses is perhaps the most effective behavioral technique of all, because it constitutes a double-edged approach. Not only is the inappropriate behavior eliminated but a correct response replaces it. Thus the child unlearns and relearns at the same time. The procedure eliminates the need for punishment and at the same time teaches correct associations.

Four principles for the teacher are:

1. *Pinpoint:* It is necessary to pinpoint explicitly the behavior that is to be eliminated or established. This takes place at many different levels relating to many differentiated academic as well as social behaviors. It leads to a hierarchical arrangement of skills and behaviors based upon expected specific behavioral objectives.

2. *Record:* This is a necessity in behavior modification and actually is what differentiates it from other techniques. Specified behaviors must be listed as they occur and thereby provide a precise record from which to proceed. The record must be accurate. If the behavior cannot in some way be measured, then one can never know if it has been established or unlearned. As maladaptive responses are eliminated, more time can then be devoted to more productive behaviors

3. *Consequate:* This unique word, which you won't find in Webster's, means "setting up the external environmental contingencies

(including primarily one's own personal responses) and proceeding with the teaching program." Contingencies include approval, disapproval, withdrawal of approval, threat of disapproval, or ignoring. Reinforcers may be words (spoken and written), expressions (facial and bodily), closeness (nearness and touching), activities (social and individual), and things (materials, food, playthings, and money). *Choice of reinforcers is an extremely important aspect of behavior modification* and constitutes an issue which should receive much discussion, debate, and criticism.

4. *Evaluate:* Evaluation should be continuous, but ultimate effects, which may be different from immediate effectiveness, must be ascertained. Hence a program must be allowed to operate for some time before final data analysis.

Values Versus Techniques

It should be apparent from the above that behavior modification represents the use of a series of scientifically verified techniques that may be used to promote more effective learning of both social and academic subject matter. A behavioral approach does not help the teacher decide why, what, and who is going to learn. These issues represent important value choices. However, after questions relating to these values have been answered, behavioral principles may be used to enhance learning of appropriate behavior. Of course, the choice of a particular technique as opposed to other approaches represents a value choice. Also, if a behavioral approach is implemented, then selection of specific behavioral procedures (e.g., approval rather than punishment), as well as choice of potential reinforcers, represents another value issue.

Opponents of behavior modification would do well to address themselves to the more important issues concerning learning rather than condemn a technique by alluding to many ancillary detriments that they feel might ensue from its application. (Generally, they make these pronouncements in the complete absence of data).

Figure 1 illustrates this point. Fill in three or four of the most important values you think should be learned by students (academic, social, or both). For example, reading, writing, consideration for others, self-actualization—whatever *you* consider to be positive. It is obvious that behavioral techniques must be used to teach "negative" as well as "positive" values.

The purpose of this exercise is to indicate that behavioral methods, much like any product of man (atomic energy, jet propulsion, governments), may be used either to the benefit or detriment of other human beings. Behavioral techniques are characterized by definitions of behavior that can be observed (pinpointed) and then measured (recorded and counted). These techniques include the isolation of specific cause and effect relationships and thereby provide a scientific methodology for the evaluation of learning.

Teaching—Art or Science?

Through trial and error, it would seem that every teacher who cares can find effective ways to stimulate students to realize their full learning potential. With or without a full understanding of behavioral principles, this teacher will find better methods of behavioral control and character development.

The ability to recognize individual differences and structure the school environment with contingencies relevant to specific situations represents an outstanding accomplishment. Good sense and good taste are important, of course. I know of one seventh-grade teacher who controlled her class by having the problem children participate in a mock wedding ceremony if they were "very, very bad." When the children evidenced proper behavior, they were allowed to "get divorced." This disciplinary procedure was tremendously effective and used behavioral principles. However, the teacher's choice of activity raises serious questions regarding the acquisition of other behaviors and attitudes. Another teacher told me of a technique she used with 8- and 9-year-old boys: "When one of the boys misbehaves, I make him wear a girl's ribbon in his hair." Does it work? Very well; but again one must question the insensitivity of this teacher to other values. It is ironic that this same person thought it "terrible" to suggest to parents that occasionally they might send their problem children to school without breakfast, in order to promote proper behavior through *rewards* of cookies, cereal, and milk.

It seems apparent that no teaching technique can be effectively divorced from the person who uses it. This point, however, makes a case for more rigorous screening of prospective teachers, not for the abandonment of effective techniques. It is a curious argument that maintains that effective techniques must be kept from teachers because then teachers may actually teach more efficiently. Because of the effectiveness of behavioral techniques, perhaps the profession may now get down to the truly important issues:

— What specifically should be learned? Or, more importantly, who will decide what is to be learned, both socially and academically? What values and accompanying behaviors evidencing selected values should be learned? When, where, and by whom?

— Who should be given the responsibility to interact purposefully in the learning process, i.e., to teach?

— Should society require any objective evidence for this learning, i.e., data from observation or other formal means?

— If continued research demonstrates the efficacy of empirical cause and effect relationships (data based on observation), ought derived principles to be systematically implemented within the schools?

— If so, then what should be the boundaries concerning choice and application of reinforcers, i.e., approval versus disapproval; punishment versus ignoring; the structuring of incompatible responses; the use of academic subject matter only as reward; social as opposed to material reinforcers. These issues represent the most important value issues within the technique of behavior modification.

Let us not waste time with such irrelevant arguments as "it's unfair." (Of course it's unfair, if unfair is defined as any individualization or discriminative assessment, e.g., differential grading.)

Then there is the charge: It's totalitarian. Nonsense! Who decides what values/behaviors should be taught to whom has nothing to do with behavior modification. Some schools are run mostly by teachers; others are controlled mostly by students. Another criticism goes something like this: Behavior mod teaches students to work for rewards. Right! Perhaps after awhile they may even find their subject matter rewarding.

Another criticism: It militates against internal control. Not so; actually, the process of partial reinforcement teaches youngsters to go for longer and longer periods of time without any external rewards. Incidentally, how long do adults maintain appropriate behavior without the occasional reinforcement from a loved one or perhaps a more tangible reward for professional behavior?

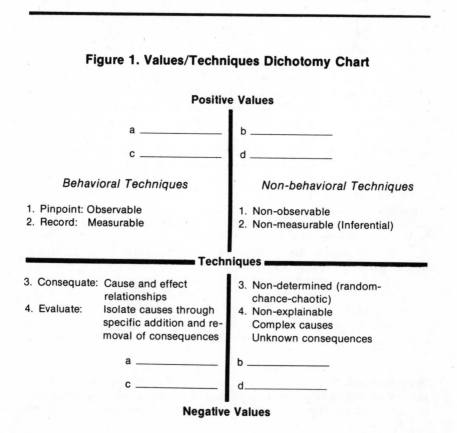

Figure 1. Values/Techniques Dichotomy Chart

Positive Values

a _____   b _____

c _____   d _____

Behavioral Techniques   *Non-behavioral Techniques*

1. Pinpoint: Observable   1. Non-observable
2. Record: Measurable   2. Non-measurable (Inferential)

Techniques

3. Consequate: Cause and effect   3. Non-determined (random-
              relationships   chance-chaotic)
4. Evaluate: Isolate causes through 4. Non-explainable
              specific addition and re-   Complex causes
              moval of consequences   Unknown consequences

a _____   b _____

c _____   d_____

Negative Values

Then it is sometimes alleged that behavior modification denies human reasoning. If anything it *teaches* human reasoning—specifying in clear, consistent, and honest ways the cause and effect relationships of life.

Another charge: *It may teach other nonspecified behaviors.* Perhaps. But let's worry about those, if indeed they exist, when there is some evidence for them. And is anyone so naive as to believe that teachers are not already approving or disapproving certain student behaviors with or without a full understanding of behavior modification?

Finally, if we cannot agree on the above, at least we may begin to take data, i.e., make systematic observations concerning what is presently going on in schools, in order to build a sounder basis for the development of teaching techniques.

It is readily apparent that, regardless of how many "behavioral recipes" are available, the insensitive teacher will still be found wanting. The art of being a good teacher seems directly related to the behaviors of that teacher as a person. Modeling effects of an outstanding individual are still among the most powerful and far-reaching of teacher influences. The truly effective teacher will combine the science of behavior with the art of living to create that exceptionally rare atmosphere: an environment where children not only take excitement from discovery but learn to be nice people.

Behavior Modification: Some Doubts and Dangers

Bryan L. Lindsey
Assistant Professor
Demonstration and Practice Laboratories
University of Georgia, Athens

James W. Cunningham
Graduate Assistant in Reading Education
at the University of Georgia and
Staff Member in an Athens Right-To-Read Program

Twelve reasons why educators should be wary

For some time "the modification of behavior" has been the textbook definition of learning, but "behavior modification" has been redefined to focus more on discipline than on intellectual growth. It seeks to mold human behavior by arranging the events in a learner's environment so that he responds in a desirable and predictable direction. These contingencies are managed by offering rewards for acceptable behavior and by withholding rewards for unacceptable behavior.

There are a number of inconsistencies in logic and some serious dangers involved in the use of behavior modification techniques in group and classroom situations. If behavior modification is used:

1. *It makes discipline a system of rewards,* which is no better than making it a system of punishments; good discipline is more than rewards and punishment; it is progress toward mutually established and worthwhile goals. A good disciplinarian is a leader who instigates and directs action toward these goals without great dependence on rewards or punishments but with an awareness of what to teach and how to teach it.

2. *It prepares students for a non-existent world;* to ignore unacceptable behavior is to socialize for an unexisting society. An important aspect of most behavior modification is to disregard, as much as possible, inappropriate behavior. Society and nature do not ignore such behavior.

Reprinted with permission from *Phi Delta Kappan*, May 1973. ® 1973 Phi Delta Kappa, Inc. All rights reserved

3. *It undermines existing internal control.* Behavior modification is a system to modify behavior in a classroom. But if students showing internal control in a class are learning, why should they be externally rewarded? Might they not then stop being self-directed and begin working only for external rewards?

4. *It is unfair.* To refrain from externally rewarding the behavior of some students for fear of weakening their internal control is to be faced with the alternative of providing rewards only for those without internal control. It will seem unfair to the students who have been doing what is expected of them without reward, while those having difficulty in doing what is expected of them are being rewarded. A point system or other reinforcement schedule shows a major weakness if allowance is made for individual differences, in that students already behaving in acceptable ways will remain unrewarded, while those exhibiting unacceptable behavior will be rewarded ("paid off") on occasions when they show modified behavior. But if no allowance is made for individual differences, students having a history of unacceptable behavior will receive fewer total rewards than those who can easily conform and obtain maximum rewards.

5. *It could instruct children to be mercenary.* A system of rewards or punishments or both requires the teacher to decide how much conformity or nonconformity is enough. Since the student is exposed to many teachers with divergent standards of behavior, he could easily become confused about what acceptable behavior is and conclude that it is whatever is profitable in a material sense.

6. *It limits the expression of student discontent.* Unacceptable classroom behavior is often an indication that content and methods used in teaching are inappropriate for the needs of students. To this extent, such behavior is healthy; it is evidence that change is in order. A system of rewards or punishments which causes students to accept instruction they should reject might make it seem less necessary to modify that instruction, and thus limit student input into the curriculum.

7. *It denies human reasoning.* Many parents and teachers treat with ridicule the practice of reasoning with children about their behavior and academic performance. But despite the obvious imperfections of man, history and contemporary times are evidence of his overall good sense and practicality. A system of rewards which would "pay" for acceptable behavior and academic effort surrenders the appeal of the reasonableness of what the child is expected to do, substituting payoffs. The denial of reason, the opposite extreme from always reasoning with children, is no less ridiculous.

8. *It teaches action/reaction principles.* The complexity of human behavior is not adequately considered, since behavior modification uses action/reaction principles where there may be no logical action/reaction pattern for the learner, but only for the teacher (manipulator). Such techniques deal with behavior in the cognitive domain when behavior should be dealt with in all domains. For behavior to be internalized, it is

best that it be understood by the individual whose behavior is being changed.

9. *It encourages students to "act" as if they are learning, in order to obtain rewards.* Once the range of acceptable behaviors is established by the teacher, the student will be able to affect responses within that range, causing the teacher to assume that desired behavior patterns are being established, when in fact the student is merely "playing the game."

10. *It emphasizes short-range rather than long-range effects.* It emphasizes to a fault the conditions under which learning is to take place rather than appropriately emphasizing what the outcome should be. This limitation results in fragmented educational experiences, and may result in long-term ill effects.

11. *It would make the student assume a passive role in his own education.* Behavior modification focuses the student's attention on behavioral responses that are acceptable by the teacher, thus limiting the choice of behaviors for the student. This could result in frustration of personal goals toward creativity and self-actualization, weakening individual motives.

12. *It is a totalitarian concept in which the behavior shown by an individual is regarded as more important than the state of affairs in the individual's life leading to his behavior.* The use of behavior modification techniques is very often an attack upon symptoms of problems rather than an attack upon problems. Because it makes teachers the sole legitimizers of classroom behavior, it gives them an "out" from really confronting the problems met in teaching children.

Behavioral Group Counseling with Disruptive Children

Jim Gumaer
School Counselor, Alachua County Schools
Gainesville, Florida

Robert D. Myrick
Professor of Education
Department of Counselor Education
University of Florida, Gainesville

Teachers work with children who "will not listen," "talk out in class," "get out of their seats at the wrong time," "do not pay attention," or "fight and disturb others." These children are labeled disruptive and are often referred to the school counselor.

A counselor's success or failure is frequently associated with his ability to work with disruptive children. One approach that has not been fully explored is behavioral group counseling. This approach makes use of client-centered and behavior modification techniques. What follows is a description of behavioral group counseling as it was used with 25 disruptive children.

The Study

Identifying the disruptive children. This study took place in an elementary school composed of grades K through 6, with a population of about 650 children. The counselor consulted with 10 teachers who had referred children with behavior problems. He clarified teacher feelings and focused on specific student behaviors such as talking out, leaving desk at inappropriate times, failing to start work on time, and hitting others. A time was arranged for the counselor to observe the children in the classroom. During the observation times he:

1. Identified possible positive reinforcers: What do the children like to do? Given a choice, what would they do?

2. Assessed the classroom learning climate: How well does the teacher relate with the children? Is the teacher's description of the situation accurate?

3. Identified subtle classroom reinforcers: Is the teacher unknowingly reinforcing the disruptive behavior by attending to it? Do the child's peers reinforce the behavior?

4. Assessed each child's potential contributions and limitations in group counseling: Is the child verbally capable? Is he socially acceptable to peers?

The counselor met with each of the 25 children. This interview provided useful information for organizing a group, including attitudes toward school, teachers, and other children and family history.

Contracting with teachers. The counselor and teachers discussed ideas for working with the children in three groups of about eight students each. A general contract was agreed on which included the time of day, day of the week, and the number of sessions that a group would meet. Each eight-week contract enabled the counselor to meet with each group for a 45-minute session one day a week.

The group sessions. The general plan that was followed consisted of objectives and a description of procedures. It provided minimum structure that helped the children become a cohesive group and focused attention on their behavior.

In the first session, the children sat in a circle and introduced themselves. The counselor explained that his work involved talking with children about feelings and things that were important to them and their teachers. After a few minutes of discussion a few children became disruptive. Some wrestled on the floor while others left their chairs to explore the room. The counselor did not intervene, but listened attentively to those who talked with him. Toward the end of the meeting in one of the groups, a fist-fight between two children took place. The counselor restrained the participants and set a limitation by saying, "No one is allowed to physically hurt another. You must talk it out."

Near the end of this session, the children were asked, "Why do you think you were selected for this group?" The children responded: "Because we're bad," "We talk out in class," "Teachers yell at us," and "We get into trouble." Some of the children became more attentive and interested in the discussion. A few wandered around the room. Several times children disrupted the discussion and became angry with one another. The counselor then emphasized another ground rule: "Everyone will have a turn to talk if we work together as a group." The group identified three behaviors that needed improvement: talking out, leaving one's chair, and being discourteous to others (e.g., making faces and laughing at others' comments).

Charting behavior. In the second group session, the counselor recorded each child's disruptive behavior. He charted the three disruptive behaviors that the group had identified. A disruptive behavior was counted as one from the time it was initiated until completed. For example, one boy left his chair and the behavior was recorded as one when he returned to his seat. However, two other types of disruptive behavior, talking out and being discourteous, were counted and recorded separately while he was out of his seat.

Behavioral data was recorded for each participant for three five-minute periods, with a one-minute interval between each period. The first five-minute period began immediately when the children arrived at the meeting place. After each session, the three behavioral categories were totaled for each child and plotted on a graph. This provided a pictorial record of group behavior.

The counselor concentrated on charting behavior and did not initiate conversation. Eventually, someone in each group asked the counselor what he was doing. The counselor explained the recording procedure, and the children usually crowded around him to look at the pad. Invariably, someone asked, "Are you going to tell on us?" The answer was "no," and the children relaxed and sat down. In all groups, the three disruptive behaviors were immediately reduced, and a discussion followed regarding who had the most marks and who had the least.

Reinforcement procedures. In the third session, each child who had less than two disruptive behaviors at the conclusion of a five-minute recording period was given two M&Ms. While distributing the M&Ms, the counselor also praised positive behaviors. For example, "Gary, you really helped the discussion by raising your hand.""John, I liked the way you waited your turn to talk."

The candy, therefore, served as a primary reinforcer for appropriate behavior, with praise as a secondary reinforcer. The primary reinforcement procedure—how candy could be earned—was explained to each group after the first reinforcement was given. By the end of the third session, all children had received both primary and secondary reinforcements for appropriate behavior.

Selected discussion topics. Charting and reinforcement procedures were continued in the next four sessions. As the children became more skilled in group discussion they also introduced topics related to their own interests and behavior, such as being sent to the principal, getting spanked, losing privileges as punishment, getting undeserved blame, and completing assignments.

The counselor frequently focused the discussion on the consequences of disruptive classroom behavior, including effects on teachers, classmates, parents, and self. Discussion was also related to precipitating events that seemed to provoke or lead to disruptive behavior (e.g., threats, dares, name calling, and boredom).

The children gradually gained more sophistication in group discussion, became more attentive, and on occasion gave personal feedback to each other. For example, "Ken, when you're talking with Bob I can't listen and understand what's going on."

The eighth meeting concluded the group sessions. Primary reinforcements were discontinued. Secondary reinforcements, however, were maintained as part of the group process. Discussion centered on a summary of previous sessions, with a look to the future. Most of the children reported that they had learned to understand themselves better. Most argeed that they were able to get along better with their classmates. All wanted to improve their behavior.

Figure 1
Graphed Mean Group Disruptive
Behavior for Three Counseling Groups

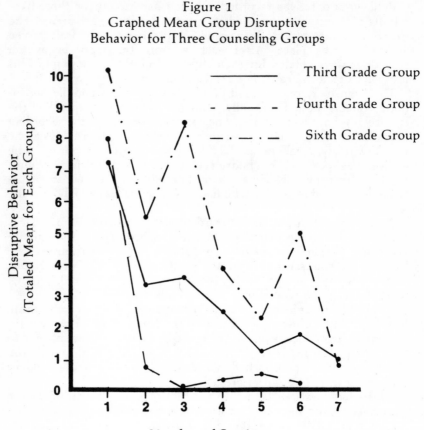

Consultation with teachers. Consultation with teachers occurred at least once per week in the morning prior to the group sessions or immediately after school. The counselor complimented teachers for their positive efforts in the classroom, and this helped establish a good working relation ship between counselor and teachers.

The counselor listened to teachers' feelings as they discussed each child's classroom behavior. Group counseling activities and progress in the group were shared, as well as classroom observations and recommendations. Teachers were encouraged to ignore some of the less disruptive behaviors (e.g., whispering and passing notes) and to reinforce with praise the positive contributions (e.g., starting work and participating in class activities).

Discussion
During the first few group counseling sessions, disruptive behavior was relatively high. In the third session, reinforcement procedures

were introduced, and the mean disruptive behavior of each group was immediately reduced. Over a period of seven weeks, the mean disruptive behavior in the group sessions for all groups diminished considerably and approached zero (Figure 1).

Reports from fourth- and sixth-grade teachers who completed pre- and post-group behavioral checklists suggested that there was a transfer of appropriate behavior to the classroom. The teacher checklist included seven behavioral items, including completes homework, turns in assignments on time, and leaves chair for non-class related activity.

Teachers from all grade levels made such comments as, "Bob has done much better in the classroom." "The group is really working; it seems to be helping Jim a lot." "Could you work with some others in my room?" "Ken and Tom handed in all their math homework this week." Other comments suggested positive differences.

It became evident, however, that the increased appropriate classroom behavior was temporary. Without group counseling and continued reinforcement in the classroom, some teachers reported that the children's behavior gradually returned to its original level about ten weeks after the study. It is possible that the effects may have been permanent if a systematic reinforcement program had continued in the classroom following counseling.

The rapid reduction of disruptive behavior both in the group and the classroom during the group counseling period increased teacher interest in the use of reinforcement techniques and demonstrated the potential value of behavioral group counseling.

Disciplinary Principles and Behavior Changing Drugs

Edward T. Ladd

The late Dr. Ladd was Professor of Education
Emory University, Atlanta

When elementary school children talk uncontrollably, run wildly about the room, fight, or have temper tantrums, the ordinary teacher or principal regards their behavior as disruptive. Such behavior can, under some conditions, be decreased by medication. It is clear that:

1. Almost any child's behavior can be toned down by a tranquilizer or barbiturate; and
2. Some of a minority of children whose motor hyperactivity or distractability results from a particular kind of clinical condition can be made to be "better behaved" by central nervous system stimulants.

This information, or a distorted version of it, has been greeted with enthusiasm by some educators and dismay by others.

Some school people have welcomed the salesman of "behavior modification drugs" to their offices; some have joined in organizations where the use of such drugs is discussed and, invevitably, promoted; some have directly approached parents of children whom they view as overactive, advising or even badgering them to get their kids put on drugs; and, according to correspondence received by the government, at least one principal has suspended a kid and refused to readmit him until that was done. Some educators have reportedly agreed to try to determine for physicians, which, if any, of their pupils have clinical hyperkinesis, so that their activity may be reduced with drugs.

Other educators, however, have expressed revulsion at the whole idea. They have opposed the drugs in letters to the press and government agencies, and one has criticized their use before a House subcommittee.

Why are educators' responses to this spreading form of medication so different, and which position, if either, is right?

Inequality in Education, June 15, 1971. Reprinted with permission of the Center for Law and Education, Harvard University.

The responses reflect in large part radically divergent approaches to school discipline, resting in turn upon divergent rationales.

The Restrictive-Punitive Rationale

Of all the many ways in which public school teachers and principals can respond to what they define as serious misbehavior, probably the commonest is to impose tight limits on the child's freedom and threaten to punish him. If one asks a school official responding this way why he does so, he is likely to offer a justification consisting essentially of these assumptions:

1. That schools should narrowly restrict the freedom of misbehaving elementary school children, because

   1a. If children are to learn what they must learn, their surroundings must be quiet and inactive;

   1b. It is essential to protect all elementary school children, obstreperous and otherwise, from injury, and to protect their "rights . . . to be secure and to be let alone";[1]

   1c. It is essential to protect school employees from any danger of injury, of theft of their belongings, and the like;[2]

   1d. It is essential to protect public property from damage, however slight, and the program of the public school from disruption; and

   1e. (It would sometimes be added) It is proper on occasion for school officials to curtail kids' freedom in the interest of satisfying or pleasing the public which the school serves.[3]

2. That—for the same reasons—violations of school norms cannot be tolerated even temporarily, but must be corrected immediately.

3. That cracking down on a misbehaving kid will tend to improve his behavior in the short run, and (often) that it will develop a pro-social self-discipline in him in the long run.

4. (Sometimes) That school officials are not bound strongly, if at all, to respect disruptive kids' rights to express themselves freely in school, their right to be protected from adult autocracy, or, if a disciplinary transfer is under consideration, their right to be educated in a regular classroom.

This battery of presuppositions might seem offhand to lend support to the use of medication to improve schoolroom behavior. How valid are they?

Conventional, orderly elementary school classrooms, it seems, are not nearly so suitable for learning as is usually believed. For one thing,

---

[1] *Tinker et al v. Des Moines Independent Community School District et al.* 393 U.S. 503 (1969) at 508.

[2] Most schools define an attack on a teacher as a more serious offense than an attack on a child. In view of children's greater vulnerability, of the fact that they are the school's clients, and of the fact that while a teacher has chosen to be in school and is paid to be there, children are forced to attend, this policy reveals an interesting sense of priorities.

[3] In a recent federal court case a principal seemed to argue that his suspension of a kid was justified in part by the need to improve the school's image and enhance the system's chances of getting school taxes raised. The court seemed sympathetic: "The . . . County School Board considered its situation serious . . . The new administration was obviously instructed to effect changes in such matters at Cedartown High which was referred to locally by some as 'Hippie Hill.' School personnel believe that the good grooming rule is necessary to change the public image of the school . . ." *Lindsey v. Guillebeau*, USDC (N.D. Ga.) Civ. Act. 2243____ F. Supp. ____ (1970).

in such classrooms a great deal of children's time, perhaps most of it, is spent in bored waiting.[4] Furthermore, there is informal evidence that while a high degree of order and quiet is essential for some particularly distractable kids, it makes other children nervous and interferes with their concentrating even on purely intellectual work: many children can learn better in a class in which a familiar level of talk and movement is allowed. There is a great deal of evidence from psychology suggesting that, in general, substantial freedom, which means at least a natural level of what adults may view as disorder, not only contributes to learning, but is a prerequisite of it, especially of the kind that might be called social or civic learning.[5] Finally, findings of the Coleman Report and other studies suggest that children in today's schools learn more from one another than from their teachers,[6] which, too, indicates that interaction between children doesn't necessarily interfere with education but more often contributes to it. Thus there is a strong case not only that Presupposition #1a is wrong, but that its opposite is true.

The correctness of each of the next three presuppositions listed is a matter of degree. Children, school employees, public property, and the school program must be protected. On the other hand, a thoroughly safe school, because it is a behaviorally antiseptic one, cannot but deprive children of opportunities for learning. The question begged by these three presuppositions is the question when protection should take precedence over opportunities for learning and when it should be the other way around. A glance at the literature of school administration and the statements of school administrators who have defended their disciplinary actions in court suggests that protection is often given absolute priority over learning. To put it differently, in our zeal to protect children from even minor dangers that are overt, we almost certainly expose them to the danger of covert but serious educational deprivation. All three of these presuppositions, at least as presently interpreted, are overstated.[7]

Assumption #1e is more questionable still. While the officials of a school district clearly have an obligation to be good stewards for the public and to cultivate the reputation of the school system entrusted to them, it doesn't seem proper for them to discharge this obligation by means which interfere at all seriously with the educational purposes for which presumably the system exists.

The assumption that a violation of a norm requires prompt attention (#2) is valid when there is a danger of harm's being continued or

[4]Philip W. Jackson, *Life in Classrooms* (New York: Holt, Rinehart and Winston, 1968), pp. 13-15.

[5]For a summary of current knowledge on this subject see Edward T. Ladd, "Allegedly Disruptive Student Behavior and the Legal Authority of Public School Officials," *Journal of Public Law*, vol. 19, no. 2 (1970), pp. 209-249.

[6]James S. Coleman *et al.*, *Equality of Educational Opportunity* (Washington: United States Department of Health, Education and Welfare, 1966), p. 22.

[7]See Ladd, *op. cit.* (note 5 above). One source of our tendency ot overprotect is the legal arrangement which makes staff members personally liable for compensation to kids who suffer injuries as a result of inadequate supervision. See Edward T. Ladd, "Students' Rights and the Need for Change in School Laws," *The Bulletin of the National Association of Secondary School Principals*, vol. 55, no. 352 (February, 1971), pp. 20-27.

increased. But everyday school life is dotted with violations which entail no such danger. For those cases the validity of Presupposition #2 hinges on that of Presupposition #3.

To move on to that presupposition, the educational value of cracking down is largely a myth. There are circumstances under which punishment deters a child from repeating a given kind of action and there are circumstances under which it does not. Fritz Redl, one of the small number of experts on school discipline, says that punishment may prevent the recurrence of a behavior if it is mild, but not too mild: if it does not confuse or cow the child but "rattles" him. George Homans writes that "punishment . . . may not have much effect on the lawbreaker" and "may under some circumstances drive [his behavior] still further away from" compliance. Certainly the most dramatic improvements in classroom behavior are brought about by "reinforcement" procedures involving no punishment at all. In the development of character and self-discipline, punishment as such seems to be of no help. Ellen P. Reese reports that it can suppress a behavior permanently only by cowing the child (the term is not hers), which is, if anything, a countereducational achievement. Students of personality development generally agree that the growth of ego controls and constructive social attitudes requires on the contrary, among other things, along with the experiencing of limits, a sympathetic environment and time.[8] Finally, B.F. Skinner warns of "an extraordinary list of unwanted by-products" punishment may have. One, of course, is the arousing of anger, which may make the disciplinary situation worse.

Presupposition #4 reflects plain ignorance: Under our legal system children do have rights to self-expression and to schooling in a regular classroom—short of their creating substantial disruption. There are constitutional as well as educational reasons why children must have freedom up to the point—a more distant point than we have believed—where it really disrupts learning.

Taken as a whole, then, the logical substructure used for justifying a generally restrictive-punitive approach is spotty: each of the presuppositions is open to question or challenge. So they can hardly be used convincingly to justify the controlling of wild schoolchildren by means of medication.

The Needs-Meeting Rationale

Because of the logical and practical weaknesses in the restrictive-punitive approach, and for other reasons, another approach is more widely recommended by educational specialists, if not so widely followed in practice, that of trying to "meet the child's needs." Those

[8]See Fritz Redl, "Management of Discipline Problems in Normal Students," in Rudolf Ekstein and Rocco L. Motto, eds., *From Learning to Love to Love of Learning: Essays on Psychoanalysis and Education* (New York: Brunner/Mazel, 1969), pp. 138-146; George C. Homans, *The Human Group* (New York: Harcourt, Brace and Company, 1950), pp. 309, 312; Merle L. Meacham and Allen E. Wiesen, *Changing Classroom Behavior: A Manual for Precision Teaching* (Scranton: International Textbook Company, 1969); Ellen P. Reese, *The Analysis of Human Operant Behavior* (Dubuque: William C. Brown, 1966), p. 47; Fritz Redl and David Wineman, *Controls from Within: Techniques for the Treatment of the Aggressive Child* (Glencoe: The Free Press, 1952); Nicholas J. Long et al., eds., *Conflict in the Classroom: The Education of Emotionally Disturbed Children* (Belmont, California: Wadsworth Publishing Company, 1960); and B. F. Skinner, "Why Teachers Fail," *Saturday Review*, vol. 48, no. 42 (October 16, 1965), p. 81.

school people who use it—whether in conjunction with the restrictive-punitive approach or by itself—hope to dry up the internal wellsprings of the behavior they disapprove. The needs they may try to meet range from mundane ones, such as those for an adequate breakfast, a comfortable desk, good ventilation, and an attractively got-up classroom or teacher, to such elusive ones as the need for success, acceptance, freedom from strong feelings of guilt, or a positive self-concept.

The rationale of this approach is derived in large measure from the mental health movement of the second quarter of the century. Its presuppositions:

1. That objectionable behavior is an abnormal, and in that sense an unnecessary, occurrence, stemming from a sickness or pathology in the child. ("There are not problem children," as a popular educational slogan has it, "only children with problems.")

2. That it is part of the job of school personnel to diagnose the unmet needs of a misbehaver, whatever they may be, and to try to meet them; and that this can be done, because

2a. Those who control schools will allow the personnel who deal with children to establish and maintain effective therapeutic or quasi-therapeutic relationships with them—as against purely didactic or autocratic ones—and to maintain these as long as there is hope that they can achieve the desired results;

2b. School personnel can and will learn to work with children in such a relationship; and

2c. Whenever school persons who thus intervene in the inner lives of children for whose behavior they have responsibility must choose between meeting the needs of the children and meeting their own needs or the demands of the school as an institution, they will stand by the children.

3. That objectionable behavior which resists elimination by this approach derives from pathology so serious as to require therapy by a specialist.

These presuppositions seem to offer the use of behavior-changing drugs for discipline stronger support. Are they more valid?

Presupposition #1, a difficult one to study, has not been systematically explored in schools. It is, however, open to obvious criticisms. If it is true, schools in the ghetto, where unmet needs are many and profound, cannot expect to cope with their discipline problems at all. A stronger objection still is that a certain amount of clashing against peers and against persons in authority may well be a normal phenomenon of healthy youth. If so, efforts to treat such clashes as a pathology to be cured by the meeting of unmet needs are likely to miss the mark entirely.

For ordinary schools, assumptions #2a, #2b, and #2c are unrealistic. Superintendents and principals, selected and trained not primarily as practicing educators or therapists but as administrators, are expected to see to it that the bureaucratic virtues of orderliness and standard-

ization prevail, and tend to press for practices which are the very an-
tithesis of what is necessary for meeting the deeper needs of individuals.[9] Only the tiniest number of our teacher training programs
are anywhere nearly as intensive as they would have to be to equip
teachers to do even low-level psychotherapy. Even many guidance
counselors are inadequately trained for such work. As to #2c, it is a
truism that if a therapist is not to subordinate his client's needs to his
own, he must be aware of his own emotional make-up to a much
greater extent than teachers generally are of theirs; and even then, if
bureaucratic pressures on him are strong, he is likely to succumb,
equate shaping the client to fit the demands of the situation with giving him therapy, and unwittingly develop rationalizations for protecting himself from knowing what he does.[10] Major therapeutic efforts
undertaken in school to improve discipline tend thus to degenerate
into brainwashing—a counter-educational procedure—if they don't
fail outright.

Yet each of the presuppositions listed has validity. Much of the
obstreperousness in school is caused by unmet needs, superficial or
deep, and teachers and counselors—sometimes even principals—do
improve behavior by meeting them.

These two approaches to discipline are the ones most school people
take, largely ignoring, incidentally, other effective approaches. The
rationale for each has serious faults, and the two are to a large extent
inconsistent.

The news that medications were available which could reduce
wildness in the classroom must have seemed to school people to be
manna from heaven, or at least to afford a Hegelian synthesis of
rationales, by offering an approach consistent with important aspects
of each. That the medications really worked seemed to suggest both
that children's behavior does need correcting and that it is pathological
and calls for treatment. The medications must have had other appeals.
They worked quickly, thus obviating the dangers about which some
people were greatly concerned. They didn't violate children's rights,
since they could be administered only by their own physicians and
with their parents' consent. And they didn't make children angry, but
tranquil, or sometimes enthusiastic.

A Third Rationale

But another line of reasoning, also coming from educators, as well
as members of the public, raised serious doubts. There was talk at a
school board meeting about drugging children "into quiet submission." At a congressional hearing on "the right to privacy," John Holt,
perhaps the most eloquent spokesman for the opposition, suggested

---

[9]For more information on, and analysis of, this situation, see American Association of School Administrators, *Professional Administrators for America's Schools: Thirty-eighth Yearbook* (Washington, the Association, 1960); and Raymond E. Callahan, *Education and the Cult of Efficiency: A Study of the Social Forces That Have Shaped the Administration of the Public Schools* (Chicago: The University of Chicago Press, 1962).

[10]See Erving Goffman, *Asylums: Essays on the Social Situation of Mental Patients and Other Inmates* (Garden City: Anchor Books, 1961).

that part of the cause of school discipline problems lay in the natural resistence of healthy kids to schools run as "maximum security prisons:" to solve these problems, schools should give children "more time and scope to make use of and work off their energy," as well as "respect, faith, hope, and trust."[11] The assumptions that dispose educators against the use of the drugs seem to be these:

1. That disciplinary troubles in school are not as serious as those school people who are restrictively and punitively oriented believe, because

    1a. A large number of so-called offenses are offenses only in that the school has defined them as such; and

    1b. Children's offenses against one another are few, and offenses against the school or its authority or property should be expected and not taken very seriously.

2. That behavioral norms in school should be liberal rather than restrictive, because

    2a. Broad experience of robust living is a necessary condition for broad learning;

    2b. Disorder and clashes between persons, habits, and preferences and so on, if appropriately handled, can provide indispensable grist for the educational mill.

3. That when a child fails to comply with a mandatory norm, school people whould respond not by forcing him to comply but by leaving him free to comply or not, showing him love, and challenging the best in him to take command, because

    3a. Every action of the school should be educational; and

    3b. A child will learn self-control and self-discipline best if he is allowed to assess situations for himself, initiate actions (rather than have to take them willy-nilly), and experience the consequences.

4. That children who misbehave have rights, and that these need more protection than do the rights of those who behave well, because the full weight of the school system is against such children, they cannot escape from its authority, and there are rarely adequate provisions for due process, to protect them from injustice.

Some of these assumptions are the opposites of others already discussed.

While presupposition #1a is patently true, #1b is not. Those close to the ghetto schools report that a continual series of misdemeanors is perpetrated by children on other children, including harassment, bullying, beating up, knifing, shaking down, and theft. Quite apart from offenses which frighten teachers off from proper performance of their duties, the offenses against children are serious enough to present a police problem which cannot be dismissed.

---

[11]Statement of John Holt in *Federal Involvement in the Use of Behavior Modification Drugs on Grammar School Children of the Right to Privacy Inquiry: Hearing Before a Subcommittee of the Committee on Operations.* House of Representatives, Ninety-first Congress, Second Session, September 29, 1970, pp. 32-33.

As has already been shown, Presuppositions #2a and #2b are essentially valid.

In the light of the police problem just mentioned, Presupposition #3a, however, seems questionable. There are many occasions in school when a child's wild behavior does not have to be stopped, and more times when it does not have to be stopped then and there, but there are times when it does. That school people with restrictive-punitive inclinations have overemphasized the school's obligation to protect other persons, the learning situation, and property, doesn't alter the fact that such an obligation exists. There are times, indeed, when it is not possible for the action taken to be educational. There is a well-accepted rule, laid down some years ago by Fritz Redl, that disciplinary action should be at least educationally neutral, not harmful; but there are occasional emergencies when that cannot be, and a certain action must still be taken even if it sets a child's education back.

Presupposition #3b is strongly supported by psychological evidence,[12] so much so that it has become a truism of school discipline that the maximum useful learning is likely to take place when a child is helped to understand any disciplinary episode in which he is involved, to interpret it in a way he finds convincing, to draw his conclusions, and to resolve what, if anything, to do about it. This means that the educator should try to prevent anything, be it strong feeling on the child's part, misinformation, or whatever, from interfering with the child's experiencing and understanding the reality he faces and having to cope with it. As a school administrator of the writer's acquaintance puts it, in disciplinary matters the monkey must be put on the child's back. The large numbers of school people who have given up hope for certain children, who have ceased trying to transfer the governance of their behavior to them, and who simply view them as "incorrigible," violate this principle but do not, of course, thereby invalidate it.

Presupposition #4 has prima facie validity. Legally, children who misbehave do have rights. And the assertions made about the threats to those rights are correct.[13] One mechanism for their protection should be mentioned as particularly relevant to the issue of psychotropic drugs. It is important, when a public official acts in a regulatory capacity, that the relationship between his actions and their effects be open and discernible. This is particularly essential in the school, where a child accused of misbehavior by a teacher lacks adult support and probably lacks neutral witnesses to whatever has happened or ensues. Children have a right to have disciplinary actions of any consequence which are taken against them be public and above board.

---

[12]See Redl and Wineman *op. cit.* (note 8 above); Ladd, *op. cit.* (note 5 above); and William Glasser, *Schools Without Failure* (New York: Harper and Row, 1969).

[13]See, for example, Ira Glasser, "Schools for Scandal: The Bill of Rights and Public Education." *Phi Delta Kappan,* vol. 51, no. 4 (December, 1969), pp. 190-194; Charles E. Silberman, *Crisis in the Classroom: The Remaking of American Education* (New York: Random House, 1970), esp. ch. 4; and Marc Libarle and Tom Seligson, *The High School Revolutionaries* (New York: Random House, 1970).

The apparent rationale, then, of the educational opponents of the drugs seems strong save for its underestimating the seriousness of disciplinary difficulties in school, and its overoptimism about the possibilities of dealing with such difficulties in educational ways. With these loopholes, it no longer seems to rule the use of psychotropic drugs out completely. Any good, loving teacher may, however reluctantly, have found it necessary to restrain a child physically, which is probably a non-educational, and possibly a countereducational thing for him to do. Might there not be circumstances which would justify his setting out to get the same purpose achieved through medication? To answer this question we must, finally, consider why and how the psychotropic drugs in question can affect children's behavior.[14]

Uses of The Behavior-Changing Drugs

Two types of drugs at issue are the tranquilizers—with which we may group the barbiturates—and the central nervous system (CNS) stimulants; all require prescriptions.

Though the tranquilizers and barbiturates are used chiefly with patients suffering from emotional or mental disorders, minor or serious, they can be effective with anyone: without permanently altering his condition, they temporarily tone down his feelings and thus reduce his activity, responsiveness, attention, and drive. When a neurotically hyperactive child is put on one of these drugs, it will probably make him less active, and if his activity has taken forms which the teacher disapproves, it will make him "better behaved." It might possibly improve his classmates' learning by reducing a distraction, or hurt it by making the classroom less lively. It will almost certainly not improve his own learning but, by making him physically less active and mentally less alert, may reduce it. Regardless of these possible effects, the parents of a neurotic child are obviously entitled to arrange for him to be given medical treatment by a responsible physician, and how that treatment is to be given is not for school personnel to say. If the effects seriously disrupted the school program, the disruption would be a matter for the school to deal with as a problem in itself.

If a tranquilizer or barbiturate is given to a neurotic child other than as part of a proper plan of treatment, or in too large a dose, or is given to a normal child, it certainly may tend to drug him "into quiet submission."

As we have seen, this is the sort of prospect that alarms those educators who oppose the drugs. But is it necessarily a bad way of dealing with a child who is unbearably wild? As we have seen, non-educational and on occasion even countereducational disciplinary measures may be in order. Isn't arranging for a child to be given a tranquilizer really more humane than many other things a teacher might properly do? The answer hinges on four subtle aspects of such a step.

---

[14]See Office of Child Development, U.S. Department of Health, Education, and Welfare, statement by panel on the use of behavior modification drugs with school children (January 1971).

First, when a teacher tries to influence a child's behavior in some standard way, he leaves the child mentally free to experience the event and to determine his response. The episode thus meets the criterion discussed above of a situation from which the child can learn. Very likely, in fact, the teacher enhances its educational potential for him by talking with him during it, so as to improve his understanding of it and strengthen his mental control over himself. Should the child's next action be unacceptable, he may, of course, encounter a new restriction. But from the beginning to the end of the episode he is allowed, and preferably helped, to apply his intelligence and will to learning what he can from it, with no barrier protecting him from reality. This would obviously be far less true if a tranquilizer were used to alter the child's interpretation of the situation he is in and his feelings about it.

Second, throughout any ordinary corrective action taken by a teacher, the relationship between his actions and their effects is rather clearly discernible to him and to anyone else who is observing. His regulatory power is used in an accountable fashion, which helps to protect the child's right to due process. This would not be the case if the teacher had somehow got the child's physician to put him on a tranquilizer.

Third, in an ordinary disciplinary episode the teacher is presumably in control of the events he has initiated and thus in a position to modify what he is doing from one moment to another, tailoring it to whatever educational needs, possibilities, or dangers may emerge. This, too, would not be so if the teacher got the child put on a tranquilizer.

Fourth, a teacher who took it upon himself to suggest that an obstreperous child be put on medication would be de facto making a tentative medical diagnosis and prescription. Even if school officials aren't forbidden by law to make tentative diagnoses or prescriptions, for them to do so would seem to be beyond their legal authority. Furthermore, insofar as school people have power of a kind which makes parents reluctant to reject their suggestions, even to make such suggestions may violate the parents' rights. This danger is not to be lightly dismissed: Public school personnel, after all, have disciplinary authority over children, influence their class assignments and grades, and may make entries on their permanent record cards, and most parents desire their favor and fear their disfavor.

It is clear, then, that however effectively tranquilizers and barbiturates might bring a public school's discipline problem under control, and however urgent might be the need to get that done, there is no place for them in public school policies or practices.

Stimulants, specifically the amphetamines, can also calm wild children down, but by a quite different mechanism. They can temporarily improve mental concentration; in therapeutic doses they can also improve some children's physical self-control.

The children with whom stimulants have these calming effects—promptly and strikingly so, by the way—are part of a small, undefined percentage of the population, possibly 5%, who, though otherwise normal and healthy, display in their early years some of the same symptoms as are shown by children with known brain injuries. The condition, commonly called "minimal brain dysfunction"—MBD—is not easy to diagnose: Specialists spend from six hours to three days on the diagnosis. Some half to three quarters of the children with MBD have inadequate control over their body movements and/or are extremely easily distracted. In either case they come across as hyperactive, and the two conditions mentioned are lumped together under the appropriate label hyperkinesis. Most children with MBD outgrow it. Meanwhile, in those of them who have hyperkinesis, the hyperkinetic symptoms of roughly half can be temporarily suppressed by stimulants, which improve their control over their responses. The effect in the classroom is that those who want to get along well with their teachers and classmates—the vast majority—become quieter and more compliant. By the same token, any who want to revolt are very likely helped to be more effective as revolutionaries.

In ordinary medical doses, then, the CNS stimulants tame only those children with hyperkinesis who respond to them and want to be tame, who are a fraction of all children with MBD, who, in turn are a fraction of all children. If given to other active or obstreperous children in medical doses, the drugs do not make such children more compliant, but may, in fact, make them more obstreperous.

Although there seems to be no danger that CNS stimulants could be used to put children into a chemical straitjacket, still, in some measure, the first of the four reasons given why school people must refrain from trying to get children put on tranquilizers may apply in the case of these drugs, too. By suppressing a mildly hyperkinetic child's symptoms, they may after all deprive him and his classmates of what may be a valuable opportunity to learn how to cope with a difficult problem. The other three reaons for people to keep hands off with the tranquilizers fully apply to the CNS stimulants as well.

Conclusion

Whatever their medical uses, behavior-changing drugs of both kinds, regardless of how well they fit with certain prevailing disciplinary assumptions, and how inadequate some of the arguments against them may be, must not be thought of as possible instruments of public school discipline.

Does this mean that schools should not be a source for the referral of children who might need just such medication? It does not. It does mean that such referrals should be treated as purely medical and not disciplinary matters.

If teachers or principals suspect that a child's objectionable behavior in school may have a medical cause, they should first examine their suspicions in the light of the fact that their responsibility for the smooth conduct of school affairs creates a possible conflict of interest which might distort their judgment and lead them to draw the line between healthy hyperactive children and hyperkinetic children in the wrong place.[15] But if in their considered judgment a child should have a medical examination, that should be recommended. *It should be recommended, though, by a school person who is not in authority over the child directly or indirectly*, and, if possible, by one who has a confidential, professional relationship to him, such as a school nurse, psychologist, or physician. School officials who are not physicians should scrupulously avoid suggesting a particular diagnosis or treatment, and all school officials should protect the confidentiality of any information concerning medical referrals or care.[16]

With these safeguards observed, it appears that in a sense the greatest concerns of both those educators who have greeted the behavior-changing drugs and those who have opposed them may be met. Used under appropriate circumstances, the drugs may, in fact, improve some children's behavior in school. Yet with school officials recognizing that their proper use is medical and not disciplinary, and acting on this recognition, the school may at the same time fully respect each child's rights to autonomy, privacy, and a broad education.

---

[15]See Edward T. Ladd, "Pills for Classroom Peace?" *Saturday Review*, vol. 53, no. 47 (November 21, 1970), pp. 66-68, 81-83.

[16]See Russell Sage Foundation, *Guidelines for the Collection, Maintenance, and Dissemination of Pupil Records* (New York: the Foundation, 1970).

Student Response to Control

In the careful method of education, the master commands and thinks that he governs, whereas it is, in fact, the pupil who governs the master. A child uses the tutor's requirements to obtain his own wishes: he always knows how to obtain eight hours' indulgence for one hours's work. . . .

Archer, R. L., editor. Jean-Jacques Rousseau: His Educational Theories Selected from Emile, Julie, and Other Writings. *Great Neck, N.Y.: Barron's Educational Series, Inc. 1964. p. 107.*

Little Brother
Is
Changing You

Farnum Gray
Educational Writer

Paul S. Graubard
Associate Professor of Education, Yeshiva University
New York

Harry Rosenberg
Director, Special Education Program
Visalia (California) Unified School District

Jess's eighth grade teachers at Visalia, California, found him frightening. Only 14 years old, he already weighed a powerful 185 pounds. He was easily the school's best athlete, but he loved fighting even more than he loved sports. His viciousness equaled his strength: he had knocked other students cold with beer bottles and chairs. Jess's catalog of infamy also included a 40-day suspension for hitting a principal with a stick, and an arrest and a two-and-a-half-year probation for assault.

Inevitably, Jess's teachers agreed that he was an incorrigible, and placed him in a class for those with behavioral problems. Had they known that he had begun secret preparations to change *their* behavior, they would have been shocked.

The New Jess

His math teacher was one of the first to encounter his new technique. Jess asked for help with a problem, and when she had finished her explanation, he looked her in the eye and said, "You really help me learn when you're nice to me." The startled teacher groped for words, and then said, "You caught on quickly." Jess smiled, "It makes me feel good when you praise me." Suddenly Jess was consistently making such statements to all of his teachers. And he would come to class early or stay late to chat with them.

Some teachers gave credit for Jess's dramatic turnaround to a special teacher and his rather mysterious class. They naturally assumed that he had done something to change Jess and his "incorrigible" classmates.

Rather than change them, the teacher had trained the students to become behavior engineers. Their parents, teachers and peers in the farm country of Visalia, California, had become their clients.

A Reward System

Behavior engineering involves the systematic use of consequences to strengthen some behaviors and to weaken others. Jess, for example, rewarded teachers with smiles and comments when they behaved as he wanted; when they were harsh, he turned away.

People often call reward systems immoral because they impose the engineer's values upon those he conditions. But the Visalia Project turns things around, according to Harry Rosenberg, head of the project and Director of Special Education for the school district. "The revolutionary thing here is that we are putting behavior-modification techniques in the hands of the learner. In the past, behavior modification has been controlled more-or-less by the Establishment. It has been demanded that the children must change to meet the goodness-of-fit of the dominant culture. We almost reverse this, putting the kid in control of those around him. It's kind of a Rogerian use of behavior modification."

Rosenberg was born and reared in Visalia and has been teacher and principal in a number of schools in that area. He began using behavior modification nine years ago, and he has kept experimentation going in the district with modest grants, mostly Federal. His proposals have emphasized that Visalia is an isolated district that, to avoid provincialism, needs contact with innovative educators from around the country. The grants have paid a variety of consultants to work with Visalia schools over the years.

Reinforcing Opponents

The idea of training kids as behavior engineers arose from a single incident with a junior-high-school student. He was in a behavior-modification program for the emotionally disturbed. His teacher told Rosenberg that although the boy was responding fairly well to the class, he was getting into fights on the playground every day. As they discussed ways of helping the boy, the teacher suggested that they identify the kids with whom he was fighting and teach him to reinforce those kids for the behaviors that he wanted. The process worked.

Rosenberg mentioned the incident to Paul Graubard of of Yeshiva University who was a consultant to the district. The incident intrigued him and he thought that training students as behavior engineers could have widespread implications in education, answering some philosophical objections to the use of behavior modification in schools.

Rosenberg had long believed that many students who were segregated in special-education classes should be reintegrated into regular classes. Graubard agreed. He designed an experiment to help children diagnosed as retardates, or as having learning or behavior problems, change their teachers' perceptions of them. This, predicted Graubard, would enable the child to be reintegrated into regular classes.

Special Classes: Incorrigibles and Deviants

For the pilot project, Rosenberg selected a local junior high school with an unfortunate but accurate reputation. It was the most resistant in the district to the integration of special-education students; it had a higher percentage of students assigned to special classes than any other in the district. Classes for those labeled incorrigible held 10 percent of the school's 450 students; Rosenberg saw this as a disturbing tendency to give up on pupils too easily. He also found that minority children were more likely to be labeled incorrigible or tagged with some other form of deviancy. Directives from the principal and supervisors to treat all children alike regardless of race or ability had failed. To make matters worse, the school also had the highest suspension and expulsion rates in the district.

Graubard and Rosenberg selected seven children, ages 12 to 15, from a class for children considered incorrigible, to be the first behavior engineers. Jess and one other child were black, two were white, and three were Chicanos. A special-education teacher gave the seven students instruction and practice in behavior modification for one 43-minute class period a day. He then moved them into regular classes for two periods each day. The teachers of these classes became their clients. The teachers ranged in age from 26 to 63, and had from two to 27 years of teaching experience.

Shaping Teachers' Behavior

Stressing the idea that the program was a scientific experiment, the special teacher required each student to keep accurate records. During the experiment, they were to record daily the number of both positive and negative contacts with their clients. The students would not try to change the teachers' behavior during the first period; instead, they would keep records only to determine the norm. For the next phase, the students were to work at shaping the teachers' behaviors and to continue to keep records. For the last phase the students were not to use any of the shaping techniques.

Rosenberg had estimated that record-keeping could begin after two weeks of training students to recognize and to record teachers' positive and negative behavior. But this preliminary training took twice as long as he expected. While the students quickly learned to score negative behavior, they were seldom able to recognize positive behavior in their teacher-clients. Without the knowledge of the teachers or of the student-engineers, trained adult aides also kept records of teacher behavior in classes. Rosenberg compared their records to those of the students to determine accuracy; he found that the aides recorded substantially more instances of positive teacher behavior than did the students. For example, an aide reported that a teacher had praised a child, but the child reported that the teacher had chewed him out. Rosenberg determined through closer monitoring that the aides were more accurate. He speculated that students were unable to recognize positive teacher behavior because they were accustomed to failure and negative treatment.

The students learned to identify positive teacher behavior accurately by role playing and by studying videotapes. This eventually brought about a high correlation between their records and those kept by adult teacher aides.

Building a New Smile

Rosenberg and Graubard taught the students various reinforcements to use in shaping their teachers' behavior. Rewards included smiling, making eye contact, and sitting up straight. They also practiced ways of praising a teacher, for example, saying, "I like to work in a room where the teacher is nice to the kids." And they learned to discourage negative teacher behavior with statements like, "It's hard for me to do good work when you're cross with me."

Each student studied techniques for making himself personally more attractive. One of the hardest tasks for Jess, for example, was learning to smile. Through use of a videotape, he learned that instead of smiling at people, he leered at them menacingly. Although he thought the process was hilarious, he practiced before the camera, and eventually developed a charming smile.

Learning to praise teachers with sincerity was difficult for the children. They were awkward and embarrassed at first, but they soon became skillful. Rosenberg said that the teachers' responses were amazing, and added that "the nonverbal cues make the difference between being a wise guy and being believable. They had to *sincerely* mean it so it would be accepted by the teacher as an honest statement of a kid's feelings, not as smarting off." Besides learning to praise and to discourage teachers, they also learned to make small talk with them. This was a new skill for these students and, after considerable training, they excelled at it.

Ah Hah!

The students enjoyed using a device that Fritz Redl, a child psychologist, has called "the Ah-Hah reaction." When a pupil was sure that he already understood a teacher's explanation, he would say that he did not understand. When the teacher was halfway through a second explanation, the pupil would exclaim, "Ah hah! Now I understand! I could never get that before." Unlike some of the other reinforcements used, this one does not directly help the teacher to improve his teaching, and it is less than honest. But it does encourage the teacher to like the student who gave him a feeling of accomplishment, and it is hoped, will lead to a better relationship between them.

Rosenberg recorded the results of the projection on a graph. It showed that during each of the five weeks of shaping, the number of positive comments from teachers increased while the number of negative comments decreased. The seven students in Jess's group felt that they had succeeded in engineering their teachers' behavior more to their liking. The "extinction" period proved to be a good indicator of the effects of this engineering. During those two weeks, there was a sharp drop in positive comments, but a marked rise in negative comments. The engineering had indeed caused the changes in teacher behavior. As the extinction period showed, the teachers were like other people. Most were backsliders and they needed persistent reinforcement to maintain their new behavior.

When the project was over, the students resumed conditioning of the teachers, but they no longer kept formal records. Positive behavior increased once again, they reported; and in many cases, the negative comments ceased entirely. Rosenberg stressed the importance of requiring the children to keep data while teaching them reinforcement techniques. Projects that do not require data have failed. A student's success with a full, formal project, on the other hand, increases his ability to continue informal use of the behavior-engineering techniques that he has learned.

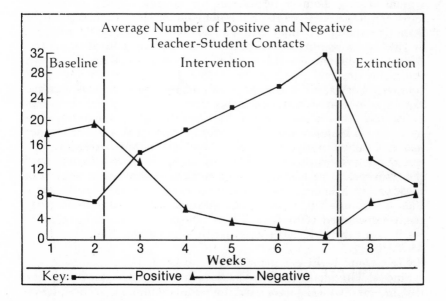

Who Really Changed?

The teacher-clients were enthusiastic about the project, and Rosenberg reported that so far, none had expressed hostility or displeasure. Some teachers did question the right of aides to observe and to record their teaching methods. But Rosenberg pointed out that it was "justified by the necessity for scientific validation of the procedure." He assured them that the district did not use data from the project for evaluation of their abilities, and so, it would not affect their careers. When he explained the project to teachers afterwards, two or three said that it did change them. They admitted that they had become more positive toward their engineers. It is interesting to note, however, that most teachers tended to think of the projects as having changed the *children* rather than themselves.

Children, especially those in special-education classes, often suffer feelings of impotence when they encounter the school environment. The crucial goal of the project was to instill within the student a feeling of power, the ability to control the controllers, i.e., his teachers and the school. As a result of their training in behavior engineering, the students reported feeling more power in their relationships with their teachers and the school than ever before. And with that feeling of power came a new feeling of self-confidence.

Parents As Clients

When children shape the behaviors of their parents, procedures are much the same as they are in the teacher-training projects. One difference, however, is that Rosenberg first asks the parents to let him work with the child. He does not tell them, though, that their children will be shaping them.

After the parents grant permission, the student decides what he wants to change in their behavior. Then, Rosenberg or a special teacher will help him to design a project to bring about that change. After the child completes his project, Rosenberg talks with the parents in their home, and tells them what the child has been trying to accomplish. For example, one girl's mother seldom had meals on time, nor did she wash or iron the girl's clothes. Through systematic use of praise and other conditioning techniques, the girl made her mother into a much better homemaker. After more than a year, the mother had maintained her improvement and gained new self-respect.

Rosenberg cited other examples of adolescents who have shaped their parents to be less restrictive. But the critical result of each of these parent-shaping projects was the parents' increased awareness of their child's needs as a person. One father said that the project had really helped them with their child; for the first time the child talked to them about the different ways that they could help him.

Switch, Don't Fight

Since children have problems with each other as well as with adults, the students at Visalia have used the same conditioning techniques on their classmates.

"We can teach kids systematically how to make friends, how to get along with other students," Rosenberg said. "If they're being teased, we can teach them how to extinguish that permanently. If they're getting in fights, we can teach them to use basic learning principles to get the same thing they were trying to get by fighting."

He cited the example of Peggy, an attractive, intelligent girl who nevertheless encountered extreme problems in school. Her sixth-grade teachers sent her to the office frequently, and she was unable to make friends with the other students, whose hostility towards her made her miserable. She was gifted academically, but apparently because of her unhappiness in school, she had never achieved even an average report card.

The special teacher helped her to design and to carry out a project to change her classmates' attitudes towards her. She was spectacularly successful. She spoke of the experience later: "They told me it was a scientific experiment, but I really didn't know what that meant. At first I was confused, and I really didn't think it would help me. But then I thought I might as well try it. At least I would get out of the classroom for part of the time."

The teacher asked Peggy to name three people whom she would like to have as friends. She named Arthur, Elwyn and Doris, all of whom frequently insulted her. For two weeks, she and her teacher recorded both positive and negative contacts with them. Then they discussed how they could increase the number of nice things that those students said to her. She began to apply the behavior-modification theory and techniques that her teacher had taught her. "I ignored Doris if she said anything bad to me. But when she said anything nice to me, I'd help her with her work, or compliment her, or sit down and ask her to do something with me. She's been increasingly saying the nice things about me and now we can ride on the bus together, and she'll sit by me in the class. I'll tell you that really helps me a lot."

She engineered Elwyn's behavior in much the same manner; she would turn her back on him whenever he said something bad to her. But the first time he walked past her without saying something bad, she gave him a big smile and said, "Hi, Elwyn, how are you today?" After he recovered from his initial shock at Peggy's overtures, he eventually became her friend.

Arthur proved to be a much tougher subject than the other two. As Peggy stated, "He calls *everybody* names. I don't think anybody likes Arthur." She attempted to ignore him whenever he called her names, but with Arthur, this tactic was unsuccessful. If the other children laughed, it just gave Arthur more encouragement. As she discussed her shaping of Arthur, Peggy showed her grasp of behavioral learning theory. She realized that the reward of the other children's laughter far outweighed her attempts to extinguish Arthur's teasing by ignoring it. They, not she, were reinforcing Arthur. She came up with a clever solution. "If Arthur was standing around with some kids, I tried to stay away from him. I'd wait until Arthur was by himself, and then I'd walk up to him, say 'Hi' and smile. He just didn't know what to do! The first time, though, he still called me a name, because he thought I was being mean to him . . .I'd never said anything nice to Arthur . . .hardly anybody ever does. I guess the only way he ever gets anybody's attention is by calling people names . . .being mean, and fighting."

Arthur was a small sixth-grader and apparently, his stature caused him a great deal of self-consciousness. Peggy continued her positive reinforcement of Arthur, who is now friendly and no longer calls her names.

Peggy's social difficulties disappeared with dramatic speed as she made use of behavior-modification techniques. The teachers who once reported her attitude as disagreeable, now found her charming and delightful. Her grade average rose to B, and the following year, she was elected president of the seventh grade.

Gifted Students

Rosenberg also instructed a class of gifted children in the use of behavior engineering; each child chose as a client a classmate, an adult, or a sibling. The children met frequently to discuss ways of handling problems and to report on the progress of their projects.

One student related how he had modified the disruptive behavior of a fellow math student. "I compliment him when he's not disruptive, and when he is, I say things to him like, 'You know, you could be a real bright student, and I like you a lot more when you don't disrupt the class.' He doesn't do it so much now, and he makes good grades."

One student was near despair over her efforts to change a teacher who, the other students agreed, was a difficult person. This teacher seemed impervious to any type of conditioning technique. "His latest thing is to send everybody out to sit under a table," she reported. "The first minute you open your mouth, he sends you out, and he doesn't really give you a chance." She had tried unsuccessfully to tell him that she was not learning math while sitting under the table, or she would apologize for saying something she should not have. But his response was usually, "You're not sorry, you're *ignorant!*" or "You're a knothead!"

The special-education teacher asked the girl to name the behavior she most wanted to change. "Sending me out without a chance," the girl replied. "That's what bothers me most. I'm out in the *first 10 minutes* of the class!"

The special teacher then suggested that she say to the problem teacher, "I'd really appreciate it if you'd give me a warning before sending me out of the room, because I have trouble about talking anyway." It was necessary for her to repeat this several times, but it wasn't long before the teacher stopped sending kids out of the room.

Dignity & Worth

In *Beyond Freedom and Dignity,* B.F. Skinner points out that "Any evidence that a person's behavior may be attributed to external circumstances seems to threaten his dignity or worth. We are not inclined to give a person credit for achievements over which he has no control."

The people at Visalia are very concerned with maintaining the dignity of their clients. They believe that dignity is lost if the reinforcements given in behavior engineering are insincere. The individual must feel that he has earned rewards by his own actions, not because the engineer is using a technique. Otherwise the gesture lacks dignity and worth.

A junior-high-school boy drew agreement from his fellow students when he said, "If the person knows you're doing it, it won't work. At least not very well. He'll figure, 'Oh, he's trying to do it on me. He's not going to change the way I am!' " The boy cited his little brother as an example. He was trying to condition him not to curse, but the child found out about the conditioning techniques, and said, "Oh, you dumb little psychologist!"

Sincerity is also an integral part of instruction in behavior engineering. Rosenberg recalled with amusement that the teachers working with him on the experiment have at times doubted each other's sincerity. "One person compliments another, who says, 'You're just reinforcing me!' And the response is, 'Oh, the hell if I am! I really mean it.' With the kids, and with our own staff," Rosenberg said, "We've had to continually stress being sincere. You should really want the other person to change."

Many of the teachers felt that the engineering by the students created a more positive working environment; it eliminated the ever-present cutting and sarcasm. It also eliminated the meanness that is so often characteristic of junior-high-school students, according to a humanities teacher. He found that children of that age often conform by being meaner than they would really like to be. "I feel these projects are very effective in giving kids an *excuse* to be positive. At this age, that seems very helpful to them."

The Visalia project revived the issue of whether it is *moral* for people to condition each other. Certainly, behavior engineering could appear to be a harbinger of *A Clockwork Orange*, or *Brave New World*. But Rosenberg, Graubard, and other behaviorists believe that people are always conditioning each other, and that often, in their ignorance, they strengthen behaviors that no one wants. Proponents believe that to make really *constructive* changes in behavior, people should be conscious of what they are doing.

Future Projects

Rosenberg envisions another three or four years of research on this project before its techniques are disseminated in the school district. The current research is to provide information for the effective matching of the student with the technique for behavioral conditioning. In the future, this "prescription" will aid the counselor in helping the student.

Additional experiments planned will compare the teacher-training effectiveness of a single child to that of two or three children working as a team. And in some projects, teachers will know that the students are trying to change them. In this instance, Rosenberg wants to find out if that will make a difference in the effectiveness of the conditioning.

Having students train teachers is inexpensive and effective. Since the students spend more time with their teachers than does any professional supervisor, they have more opportunity to change them. Students also have the most to gain or to lose from the quality of teaching. Rosenberg estimates that the students are doing about as well in exercising control over human behavior as professionals who charge 50 dollars an hour.

Games Teachers Play

Leslie Chamberlain and Morris Weinberger

Professors of Educational Administration and Supervision
Bowling Green State University, Ohio

Although there are differences of opinion concerning classroom control and methods for achieving it, all teachers will agree that a pleasant, well-disciplined classroom atmosphere results in more effective learning for all. Good teachers realize that to a very large extent they themselves create the climate in their classrooms. But even a good teacher may play classroom "games" that lead to pupil boredom and disinterest, and result in behavior problems.

The game of ambiguous rules, for example, is a common cause of classroom disturbance. Teacher and pupils learn the rules and then spend hours playing the game with repeated student testing to make the rules specific. In "How wide is an aisle?" for example, the students' team "scores" whenever there is a foot in the aisle without reprimand and the teacher "scores" when he catches someone. Repeated trials by students, with a scolding each time ("get your foot out of the aisle"), result in both sides' eventually agreeing on an imaginary line that is the boundary. A foot inside or on the line is acceptable but one-quarter inch over is not. This game may take an hour to play on a day early in the fall but is played more quickly when students reopen the game out of boredom in the spring. Similar games are "But you've been to the bathroom" (a game more often won by students) and "When is a pencil dull?" (a game the teacher usually wins).

Uncritical enforcement of traditional rules is another cause of classroom misbehavior. Too often teachers perpetuate rules without knowing why they do so, what purpose the rules serve, or what the total effect of the rule is on either the class as a whole or an individual student.

Among the most common classroom "games" are the teacher's attitudes and behavior. Children behave much like the adults around them. While it is flattering to have a student imitate him, the teacher must realize that anything he does before children, for good or ill, remains with them longer than most adults realize. Though a teacher may recognize the pupil imitations of his virtues, it is much more difficult to recognize faults secondhand, and he may be using a teaching technique which has become a disciplinary pitfall and the cause of problem after problem. Flippant remarks, sarcasm, and unfriendly looks are often unconsciously used in teaching. A person who is truly objective will notice antagonistic or belligerent pupil feedback, but many teachers fail to recognize it. When one *knows* one is right, it is hard to hear or see contradictory evidence.

The art of listening is not to be taken lightly, for this is how the teacher interprets what people, especially his students, are trying to tell him. Unfortunately, most teachers feel they are listening when they are only hearing the words. Listening involves understanding from the speaker's viewpoint, a detail often missed by even good teachers. Teaching involves the interactions of human beings and a good teacher learns from what he hears as well as from what he sees.

Teachers should also realize that the life goals of children and of adults are usually different, and that children of different ages have different goals. A student's actions should be evaluated in terms of the individual or group goal being sought at the time. A student will select from his different behavioral patterns the actions he believes will help him to achieve his personal goal and then behave accordingly. Teachers who learn to adjust their thinking to what is appropriate student behavior in terms of the child's age and his goals will seldom need to apply external controls. Failure to see this viewpoint means that the teacher will be out of step with his class most of the time, and have many disciplinary situations.

Using the lecture method is a pitfall for many beginning teachers. It often fails to meet the interest, needs, and abilities of the students. Yet a lecture can be an efficient technique occasionally, if the content is at the children's level of understanding, is adapted to student needs and goals, and is brief. A teacher who comes to class poorly prepared, with a bare minimum of correct information, and no thought of its interest level, should hardly be surprised when the students fail to pay the rapt attention he would like.

Too many people believe that a knowledge of subject matter is nearly all of the professional preparation required to teach. This point of view defines learning as the mere acquisition of factual knowledge. But learning affects not only factual knowledge but habits, understandings, attitudes, emotional control techniques, and social values as well. In fact, learning to like to learn may be the most important thing a teacher can help a student acquire.

Some problems develop from the way a teacher implements his teaching. Classwork that is too advanced, too verbal, or in a poorly planned sequence will create difficult situations for both the teacher and the students. Behavior standards that are too high or too low, or a classroom that has too much or too little organization, may result in boredom or fatigue.

An important factor affecting the environment of every classroom today is the increased emphasis on education. Students are expected to read more, study more, write more, and learn more. The problems posed by this pressure are creating anxiety and additional indirect disciplinary pressures within the classroom. It takes conscious effort and constant readjustment for even experienced teachers to match their teaching to student needs, abilities, interests, and time.

Many problems of discipline are actually responses to inadvertent teacher behavior. Difficult as self-assessment always is, a conscientious teacher will examine his day-to-day habits with care, to make certain that what he calls student misbehavior isn't really his, and to understand the behavior games that he and his students play.

The Ripple Effect in Discipline

Jacob S. Kounin
Paul V. Gump

Wayne State University, Detroit, Michigan

Discipline is a serious concern to many teachers, especially beginners. The teacher who seeks help in discipline is likely to get advice that draws heavily on lore. The counsel may carry the name of a respected authority or the prestige of a widely accepted educational philosophy.

But how much advice on classroom discipline, even advice offered under such auspices, meets the test of experimentation? How many widely accepted beliefs and practices have been upheld by careful research?

In Detroit, we are studying classroom management.[1] In one phase of our study, we are paying special attention to the "ripple effect," or the influence that control techniques have—not on the children who are being disciplined—but on the other children who are watching and listening.

Briefly, the problem may be put in this way: While the teacher is correcting Sally, what effect is the disciplinary measure having on Ruth, who is sitting nearby, taking in what is happening?

Answers were sought in the kindergartens of twenty-six representative Detroit schools. In the study reported here, fifty-one undergraduates served as observers. The students began their observations on the first days of the new school year.

The observers were carefully instructed on their assignment. They were to note any incident in which a kindergartner watched the teacher correct another child for misbehavior. They were to report in detail on three phases of each incident: the behavior of the watching child immediately before the incident, the behavior of the teacher and

[1] The research is sponsored by the Department of Educational Psychology, College of Education, Wayne State University. Financial support has been provided by the National Institute of Mental Health, National Institutes of Health, Public Health Service, Grant 1066.

the child who was being corrected during the incident, and the behavior of the watching child for two minutes after the incident.

Four hundred and six such incidents were analyzed. In our analysis, we classified the control technique itself, the behavior of the watching child before the incident, and the behavior of the watching child after the incident.

The control technique

Three dimensions of the control techniques used by the teachers were measured: clarity, firmness, and roughness.

Clarity involved the teacher's directions to the children. How clearly did the directions define the misbehavior the teacher wanted to bring to an end?

A teacher might say: "Tommy, stop it!" Or "Tommy, you can't do that!" Or "Tommy, that will do!" However emphatically uttered, these directions did not make it clear what Tommy was to stop doing.

A teacher who wanted to make sure that a pupil understood what was expected of him might use one of several approaches. The teacher might give directions that defined the pupil's misbehavior: "Tommy, don't take the blocks away from Johnny while he's using them." Or the teacher might give the child an acceptable standard of behavior: "Tommy, in kindergarten we ask for things. We don't grab." Or the teacher might tell Tommy how to stop the misbehavior: "Tommy, put those blocks down and look at the picture books."

Firmness involved how much "I-mean-it" the teacher packed into the disciplinary technique. How did the teachers say "I mean it"?

By touching or guiding the child. By speaking emphatically. By walking close to the child. Or by following through, that is, by focusing steadily on the misbehaving child until he conformed. If the teacher brushed over the trouble lightly, the correction conveyed little firmness.

Roughness described techniques in which the teacher expressed hostility or exasperation. If the teacher touched the child, the touch had more pressure than was necessary. If the teacher gave the child a warning look, the look was angry rather than serious. The samples in the study showed no extremely harsh techniques. No child, for example, was shaken or spanked.

The children's reactions

The children who watched while a classmate was being corrected responded in various ways, which we classified in five categories. Sometimes boys and girls showed no reaction. They simply went about their business, making no observable response to the episode. If the children happened to be drawing when a classmate was admonished, they simply continued with their drawing.

At other times, children reacted sharply to the correction of a classmate. They lost interest in what they had been doing and became worried, confused, and restless. This type of reaction was classified under "behavior disruption."

At still other times, children responded with a special effort to be good. They stopped a misbehavior of their own, sat up taller, paid closer attention to the lesson, or tried in some other way to show that they were not misbehaving. These reactions were grouped under "conformance."

Sometimes the correction had no deterrent effect whatsoever. Even though a child had just seen a classmate corrected for misbehaving, he launched some mischief of his own. This response was classified as "non-conformance."

At times, children in the audience vacillated between conformance and non-conformance. During the two minutes after the teacher had corrected a classmate, they both conformed and misbehaved.

We related the children's reactions to the teachers' control techniques.[2] When the teachers made it very clear what they expected of a child, the children in the audience responded with increased conformance and decreased non-conformance. When the teachers did not make it clear what they expected of the child they were correcting, the effect on the young observers was reversed, that is, they responded with less conformance and more non-conformance. The probability level[3] for this difference, by the chi-square test, was .01.

The clarity of the teachers' directions was plainly related to the responses of the children in the audience, but the firmness of the teachers' technique, the researchers found, only tended to be related to the reactions of these children. In other words, the knowledge that a control technique was firm or lacking in firmness did not enable us to predict how a watching child would react.

Finally, we found a relation between the roughness of the control technique and the response of the watching child. Roughness did not lead to increased conformance and decreased non-conformance. Instead, rough techniques were followed by an increase in behavior disruption. Severe techniques did not make for "better" behavior in the watching child. Severe techniques simply upset him.

Our study recognized that control techniques alone do not determine how a watching child reacts. Other influences are also at work.

The impact of the setting

We investigated three possibilities. First of all, we asked: "What was the watching child doing just before the incident?" Our next concern: Was the watching child psychologically close to the child who was being corrected? Was the child in the audience watching his misbehaving classmate with considerable interest? Finally, how long had the watching child been in kindergarten?

---

[2]The inter-coder reliability on a 24-item control technique code was 78 per cent agreement; on a 34-item audience reaction code, 83 per cent. Since the former was collapsed to three dimensions and the latter to five categories, the functional reliability would be even higher. To avoid possible bias, different teams coded the control techniques used by teachers and the reactions of the watching children.

[3]Probability levels refer to the probability that the differences obtained could be due to chance. For example, a probability level of .01 means that the difference obtained would occur by chance less than one time in a hundred.

Children who were themselves misbehaving—or even innocently related to misbehavior—were much more responsive as they watched the teachers' efforts to control than were the children who were free of any connection with misbehavior. Children who at the moment were free of misbehavior were quite likely to show no reaction. Children who were misbehaving showed more conformance, more non-conformance, and markedly more vacillation between conformance and non-conformance (probability level .001)

It was instructive to compare the effects of clarity and firmness on the various groups. The effects already noted for clarity were obtained regardless of whether or not the watching child was associated with misbehavior. However, firmness affected only groups that had some connection with misbehavior. In these groups, high firmness increased conformance and decreased non-conformance (probability level .05).

The length of time the children had been in kindergarten, we found, affected their reactions. On the first day the children were highly sensitive to control techniques. They showed some outward reaction to 55 per cent of all control incidents. On the next three days they reacted outwardly to only 34 per cent of the incidents (probability level .001).

Among our findings

To the extent that we can generalize on cause and effect, the study indicates that the reaction of watching children to a teacher's control of a misbehaving child is related to at least three factors.

First, the newness of the situation. On the first day in kindergarten, watching children showed the strongest responses.

Second, the behavior of the watching children. Pupils who were themselves misbehaving or interested in children who were misbehaving were more likely to show the strongest reactions; the particular response was most likely to be vacillation.

Third, the disciplinary technique itself, that is, the clarity, the firmness, and the roughness of the technique.

When the teacher made it clear what behavior she objected to or what behavior she expected, the watching children responded with increased conformance and decreased non-conformance.

If the teacher's behavior conveyed firmness, the watching children sometimes responded with increased conformance and decreased non-conformance. This reaction occurred if the watching children had been misbehaving or interested in a child who was misbehaving.

If the teacher used rough techniques, the children showed behavior disruption but not conformance or non-conformance.

It should be kept in mind that clarity in the teacher's directions led to greater conformance and less non-conformance in a new and unstructured situation. When children are new to kindergarten or to the teacher, they may be especially sensitive to his directions and desires. As the child feels more at home in kindergarten and more at ease with the teacher, we would expect clarity to be less important. Several studies are now in progress to check this expectation.

Fact and lore

What meaning does the study have for teachers of children who are just beginning kindergarten? It is clear that a ripple effect does exist. What a teacher does to control children's behavior affects the children who watch as well as the children who are corrected.

The teacher who is interested in controlling ripple effects can generally do so best by giving clear instructions to the child rather than by exerting pressure on him. However, some intensity or firmness is effective if the children who are watching are themselves inclined to "deviancy."

The study does not support the notion that the teacher must "bear down" on the first day or "make an example" of a child. Such steps are not necessary to induce conformity in children who are entering kindergarten. Nor does the study support the contention that roughness and anger are simply firmness intensified. Firmness and roughness are different qualities. Witness the different effects they have on watching children.

Special Issues Today

Investing In Youth:
An Approach to Discipline
in Urban Schools

Robert L. Green

Dean, College of Urban Development
Professor, Educational Psychology
Michigan State University
East Lansing

Janet Brydon

Research Associate and Editorial Consultant
College of Urban Development
Michigan State University
East Lansing

Unemployment, poverty, crime, and other societal problems adversely affect the quality of education in our schools. Children from low-income neighborhoods or urban areas of high unemployment are often confronted in the classroom by teachers who view them as "intellectually deprived" and unlikely to succeed educationally.

These teachers, and also the administrators of many schools in poor, highly urbanized areas, find themselves becoming more occupied with being property managers or caretakers than with meeting children's needs. Such teacher/educator apathy toward education inhibits the school's learning climate, decreasing the student's motivation to learn. Intellectual and emotional development often become dormant. Scholastic achievement at a high level does not occur, discipline problems develop, and ultimately, bored and frustrated students, with excellent potential for educational growth, drop out of school.

Educational dormancy is detrimental to the growth of our society. John Dewey (3, pp. 104-105) attributes to Plato:

An individual is happy and society well-off when each individual engages in those activities for which he has natural equipment. The primary office

107

of education is to discover this equipment to its possessor and train him for its effective use.

Dewey (4, p. 7) himself describes the school as a place where individualism and socialism are one: "Only by being true to the full growth of all individuals who make it up, can society by chance be true to itself."

The educational system can be a valuable tool for solving urban social problems and improving the quality of life for the poor. Teachers and school administrators must see that social conditions in many urban neighborhoods are not permitted to stymie the education of American youth.

Race, Social Class and Nonachievement

The educator plays a key role in determining the direction of U.S. education. The teacher's or administrator's attitude toward school children can swing the balance toward educational growth or stagnation.

Robert Rosenthal (10) maintains that teachers devote more time and attention to children they have favorable attitudes toward, and these favored children tend to learn more. W. Victor Beez's (10, p. 62) work with 60 Headstart preschoolers and 60 Headstart teachers supports Rosenthal's theory. Beez told 30 teachers to expect below-average work from their "below average" children. The others were told to expect above-average work from their "exceptional" children. Observers who were unaware of the teacher's expectations noted that teachers worked much harder when they believed they were teaching a bright child.

Unfortunately teachers tend to have greater expectations for middle-income than for low-income children. Eleanor Leacock (10, p. 63) studied four schools in two poor and two middle-income neighborhoods and found that teachers' attitudes were much more favorable toward middle-income children than toward low-income children. When racial prejudice is added to social class bias, the effect on children is even more disastrous. Leacock found that 43 percent of teachers' comments about Black children were negative as opposed to 17 percent of comments about white children.

There are many subtle ways in which negative attitudes toward poor, Black children can work against these children. One of the most prevalent is the misuse of standardized intelligence or achievement tests. The scores which children make on these tests are frequently taken as absolute measures of ability rather than only indicators of current educational status influenced by environmental conditions. On the basis of test scores many poor children are placed in "tracks" or achievement groups that limit their learning opportunities and consequently their future. Most standardized tests are designed by white male Ph. D's with middle- or upper-income backgrounds. These men are often insensitive to the culture, lifestyle and societal forces that affect the academic performance of low-income children. When children fail the IQ test it is most likely because the questions are not related to their realm of experience. (5, p. 72)

Negative attitudes toward low-income Black children also may be manifested in overtly discriminatory behavior. For example, many administrators in majority-Black or newly-desegregated schools feel they must institute rigid rules to keep students under control. These rules are usually enforced unequally with Blacks being penalized more severely than whites for breaking them.

Phil Kaplan (12, p. 19) a Little Rock, Arkansas, lawyer active in civil rights cases, cites examples of Black students being suspended for wearing Afro-type hair styles, getting married, being disrespectful, and questioning a teacher's authority.

Specific examples of overt discrimination against students are enumerated in *The Student Pushout* (12, pp. 14-15):

A high school junior in South Carolina told of a fighting incident between a Black and a white student in her school. The Black student was expelled and had to appear in court. The white student was not expelled.

Other students were suspended for "talking to a white girl," for "going with a white girl and sitting and talking with her on the lawn," for "eating lunch on the white side of the lunchroom."

Overt discrimination has also been directed toward Black teachers. The National Education Association (9, p. 4) estimated the number of Black teachers displaced from jobs in 17 Southern and Border states to be 39,386 in 1972, an increase of 6,490 over 1970. A Race Relations Information Center Report (6, p.1) tells that a Black male with 25 years experience as a principal was assigned to teach seventh-grade social studies and history. It tells that a home economics teacher with 23 years experience was fired for "incompetence" five days after signing her new contract to teach second grade. If Black adults are abused in such a way, it follows that children who are more defenseless will be even more abused.

Need for Active Learning

The dismissal or demotion of Black teachers and administrators may have far-reaching effects on Black and other minority children, contributing to their miseducation. When those who understand the problems and the attitudes of Black youth are replaced by less-qualified teachers perhaps not familiar with the needs of these young people, rules are frequently set up to "keep the situation under control." The educational structure becomes more rigid, interaction among students is minimized, and curiosity discouraged.

In *Crisis in the Classroom*, Charles Silberman (11, p. 128) describes an elementary school principal lecturing to a student assembly about the wonders of a school for the "deaf and dumb." The silence was wonderful, he told the assembly; it helped the children get their work done. This principal's goal apparently was to turn normal children into youngsters behaving as though they were missing two of their faculties.

Silberman (11, p. 135) also cites the following editorial which a principal censored from a fifth grade newspaper:

Many of us feel strongly that we have a lack of freedom in school. Maybe adults don't realize what it feels like to be ten or eleven or twelve years old and have to ask permission to go to the bathroom or to throw away a piece of paper, or to talk to a teacher. When we are not permitted to leave our seats to go to the project area or the library we know you are saying you don't trust us.

Teachers may be thinking, "If we give you this freedom you will just be noisy and fight." But if students had more freedom we would also accept more responsibility.

School would be a more pleasant place for all of us if there weren't so many unnecessary rules . . . .

Some teachers and administrators are beginning to realize that learning is an active process, physically as well as mentally. Talk and motion in the classroom can be productive. In recent years new schools have been designed with numerous workshop areas where students may choose their activities and engage in an active learning process. This flexibility, however, usually is restricted to affluent areas, while rigid teaching practices often are retained in central urban areas.

It is the teacher's responsibility to help students become independent human beings, relying on their own resources. This means helping children assume responsibility and develop self-control.

Staten Webster (16, p. 5) states:

Self-control cannot be learned in a vacuum. Students must be provided with opportunities to participate in making decisions about those things which control their behavior. True self-discipline cannot be learned if all restraints are super-imposed from without. Whenever possible, students must have the opportunity to set limits and to choose from behavioral alternatives if they are to learn personal control.

Irrelevant, Outmoded Curriculum

In addition to being restricted to their desks and forbidden to speak, children are frequently subjected to outdated curricula which they cannot relate to their personal experiences or to the world around them.

Most social studies texts, for instance, are outdated before they leave the press. Social conditions around the world are changing so rapidly that today's news conflicts with textbook facts. Also, many textbooks distort factual information, underrepresenting some aspects of a particular subject and overstressing others. It is well known that for many years textbooks scarcely recognized that Blacks existed at all in American society. Traditional curricula, relating only to the white, middle-income experience, transmitted very negative perceptions to minority and poor children, fostering doubts and anxieties about their cultures and backgrounds. (1, p. 29)

Educational relevancy is tied to social conditions. Young people want to know about Watergate, hunger, poverty, crime, and the fair administration of justice. Learning should focus on broad principles, then reach out for meaningful, timely examples to illustrate those principles. The teacher should be a well-informed resource person, developing, if necessary, her/his own curricular materials to meet the needs of a particular learning situation.

Instead of expanding existing student interest in a subject, teachers frequently adhere to rigid course and curriculum outlines. Ignoring student's ideas and interests dampens their enthusiasm and makes them feel inadequate or unimportant. Silberman (11, p. 125) cites the following example of inflexibility in lesson planning and course content:

> A scholar studying curriculum reform visits a classroom using a new elementary science curriculum. Arriving a few minutes before the class was scheduled to begin, he sees a cluster of excited children examining a turtle with enormous fascination and intensity. "Now children, put away the turtle," the teacher insists. "We're going to have our science lesson." The lesson is on crabs. (11, p. 125)

Testing and Self-Esteem

The constant testing and evaluation that students undergo as part of their educational experience also can help destroy their self-respect. Some educators (11, p. 138) have made it clear to students that the purpose of this evaluation is rating: "to produce grades that enable administrators to rate and sort children, to categorize them so rigidly that they can rarely escape." Rigid testing, with the goal of grouping or "tracking," dooms children to curriculum that is noneducative and limits later opportunities in life. Benjamin Bloom (11, p. 139) describes this rigid rating system as "the most wasteful and destructive aspect of the present educational system," reducing learning motivation and destroying the self-esteem of large numbers of students.

Rebels

It is no wonder that discipline problems crop up in such a repressive school climate. Perhaps it is a healthy sign that larger and larger numbers of students are speaking out and acting against a system which humiliates and degrades them.

Thinking, active minds often question a teacher's opinion or occasionally forget a boring homework assignment. Students sometimes wear clothing or hairstyles which conflict with rigid dress codes. Teachers frequently interpret such behavior as disrespectful or insubordinate. Rather than looking to the system for the root of the problem, the teacher finds fault with the students. Studies have shown that an increasing number of young people are being suspended for such behavior and the majority of suspended students are Black.

In Little Rock, Arkansas, (12, p. 2) in 1968-69, with very little desegregation, there were 1,329 suspensions, 62.9 percent of them Black. In 1971-72, the first year of major desegregation in Little Rock, there were 1,881 suspensions, with 79.9 percent being Black. The unequal distribution of suspensions by race indicates that racial conflict and hostility were major factors in the handling of behavior. In most of these cases a very extreme discipline measure was chosen to deal with a situation that could have been resolved by understanding and increased communication. In effect, students are pushed out of school because of prejudice and discrimination.

Restrained and alienated by the system, other students drop out before they are pushed out. These youngsters usually are so bored or frustrated with school that they just stop coming. Frequently they're behind their age group, they feel backward or slow and fear they will never catch up. (8)

In 1972, 800,000 students dropped out of high school in the U.S. (13, p. iii) The number of dropouts in New York City alone increased by 10 percent from 1963 to 1973. (17, p. 43)

The dropout gives the teacher one less "discipline" problem with which to deal; however, high unemployment among unskilled laborers and low pay in jobs available to dropouts may increase the dropout's level of frustration, creating greater problems for the dropout and for the society upon which she/he is dependent.

Recommendations

The actions of "discipline problem" students "may simply be a form of protest against the futility or the inevitability of an education which they do not see as either relevant or important in terms of their life goals." (7, p. 70)

Our public schools need not be prisons for our children's minds and bodies. Poor social conditions in urban neighborhoods need not dictate a low quality of education and low-learning levels. Brookover, et. al., (2, pp. 95, 102-103) have identified several urban schools in neighborhoods with low socio-economic status where students are high achievers.

One of these, a predominantly Black school in Mount Clemens, Michigan, has a highly structured environment, yet students are encouraged to contribute their thoughts to the class discussion. Teachers do not believe that a student's past determines future achievement, and parent support of the academic program is strong. Both students and teachers exhibit a very low sense of futility.

Another example cited, a high achieving, predominatly poor white school, also maintained a good relationship with the community and had strong parental support.

The above two cases indicate that low income and race need not determine the achievement level of children. Educational stagnation can be alleviated and the number of suspensions, dropouts, and other discipline problems can be reduced.

One of the most significant ways of improving the quality of education and reducing racial, ethnic, and income bias, is to revamp many of the existing teacher and school counselor training programs. Many traditional programs prepare teachers and counselors to deal only with children who have backgrounds similar to their own, i.e., white and middle-income. These professionals, when placed in urban schools in low-income neighborhoods, find it unsatisfying to advise poor, minority children. Teacher and counselor training programs must strive to give urban teachers and counselors an understanding of the needs of inner-city children. Including urban development and minority studies classes in teacher and counselor training curricula may help fill this need.

Curriculum reform is also needed in our school system. Educators must seek to make the subject matter as meaningful as possible for the student. Social conditions, student background, and student interests should all be considered when planning courses.

Blacks, Native Americans, and Spanish-speaking people should be given fair representation in text books and curricula, and educators should keep informed of new multiracial educational materials. Universities can help. For example, the Michigan State University Urban Affairs Library has developed a multiethnic children's book collection to help teachers and future teachers choose between high and low quality multiethnic reading material. A critical review accompanies each book to aid the teacher in her/his evaluation.

Advocacy

In recent years civil rights organizations have become concerned with student rights. The NAACP, for example, has defended in court numerous students who were unfairly dismissed from school or otherwise mistreated in school.

The Children's Defense Fund (founded in 1973) uses litigation, efforts of community organizations, and investigative and evaluative research to protect and advance the rights of our nation's children.

Teachers and administrators must become advocates for children who cannot defend themselves. Educators must push for constructive changes in the educational, political, and social sectors to benefit their students. In the past few years teacher unions have been founded to safeguard teachers' rights. In 1972, there were 145 teacher strikes in the U.S. (15) During the first few days of September 1973, an estimated 25,000 teachers walked out interrupting the education of 750,000 youngsters. (14, p. 80) How many teachers would go on strike in support of their students' rights?

It has often been said that young people constitute our nation's greatest resource. If this is true, we have been ignoring a large portion of our wealth. Often minority young people from low-income neighborhoods and areas of high unemployment are not counted among our future leaders. The consideration we give now to their education will help determine the quality of life for the next generation. By investing in all our youth, we are investing in a better future for all Americans.

REFERENCES

1. Aragon, John. "Alienation in the Schools: The Unwanted, Excluded, and Uninvolved." *Student Displacement/Exclusion: Violations of Civil and Human Rights.* Report of the Eleventh National NEA Con-

ference on Civil and Human Rights in Education. Washington, D.C.: National Education Association, 1973. pp. 29-35.

2. Brookover, Wilbur B., and others. *Elementary School Social Environment and School Achievement.* Final Report of Cooperative Research Project No. 1-E-107. East Lansing: Michigan State University, College of Urban Development, July 1973. 203 pp.

3. Dewey, John. *Democracy and Education.* New York: Macmillan Company, 1916. 434 pp.

4. _____ "The School and Social Progress." *The School and Society.* Chicago: University of Chicago Press, 1900. pp. 6-29.

5. Green, Robert L. "The Awesome Danger of 'Intelligence' Tests." *Ebony* 29: 68-70, 72; August 1974.

6. Hooker, Robert W. *Displacement of Black Teachers in the Eleven Southern States.* Nashville, Tenn.: Race Relations Information Center, December 1970.

7. Jessup, Michael H., and Kiley, Margaret A. *Discipline: Positive Attitudes for Learning.* Englewood Cliffs, N.J.: Prentice-Hall, Inc., 1971. 156 pp.

8. Motz, Annabelle B., and Weber, George H. "On Becoming a Dropout." *Phylon* 30: 1-14; Summer 1969.

9. National Education Association. "Discrimination Has Cost Minority Educators over 200,000 Jobs, NEA Official Asserts." Press release. October 19, 1973. 5 pp.

10. Rosenthal, Robert. "The Pygmalion Effect Lives." *Psychology Today* 7: 57-63; September 1973.

11. Silberman, Charles E. *Crisis in the Classroom: The Remaking of American Education.* New York: Random House, Inc., 1970. 553 pp.

12. Southern Regional Council and the Robert F. Kennedy Memorial. *The Student Pushout, Victim of Continued Resistence to Desegregation.* Atlanta: the Council, 1973. 83 pp.

13. U.S. Department of Health, Education and Welfare, Office of Education. *Positive Approaches to Dropout Prevention.* DHEW Publication No. (OE) 73-12300. Washington, D.C.: Government Printing Office, 1973. 89 pp.

14. U.S. News & World Report. "Back to School and a Raft of Problems." *U.S. News & World Report* 75: 80-81; September 17, 1973.

15. _____ "Striking Teachers Find Rough Going." *U.S. News & World Report* 73: 85; September 18, 1972.

16. Webster, Staten W. *Discipline in the Classroom.* San Francisco: Chandler Publishing Company, 1968. 142 pp.

17. Weissman, Seymour. "Dividends for the Forceouts: Despair, Drugs, Delinquency, Detention." *Student Displacement/Exclusion: Violations of Civil and Human Rights.* Report of the Eleventh National NEA Conference on Civil and Human Rights in Education. Washington, D.C.: National Education Association, 1973. pp 43-47.

Law and Order and Race in the Classroom

Melvin P. Sikes

Professor of Educational Psychology
University of Texas

Discipline has always been a major consideration in the area of classroom management. Cheating, talkativeness, and fighting have come to be seen as a part of the overall educational process. Channeling misdirected energies into productive behaviors has become almost as great a challenge to the teacher as passing on a fund of special information. Despite its seeming persistence in the classroom setting, misbehavior should not be taken lightly, for the school as socializing agent has a responsibility in shaping the character of its charges.

Since the mid-sixties there has been a rapid change in the type of disciplinary problems in the schools. Increasing numbers of these problems are interlaced with racial overtones. It appears that some actually are racial in nature while others have race as an improperly injected factor. In view of what seems to be a worsening racial climate in our schools, it behooves us to take a closer look at this potentially explosive situation. No one can benefit in a school atmosphere of tension, fear, distrust, and hostility. This is true of administrator, teacher, and student. This is true regardless of the race or ethnicity of the individual. Some insights into the overall race-related discipline problem may stimulate further exploration and examination while suggesting remedial approaches to the situation.

Historical Perspectives

Problems stemming from desegregation seem to be the basis for most racial strife. Prior to the 1954 Supreme Court Brown Decision, disciplinary problems appeared to have no color. That is: stealing, cheating, fighting, and the like could be found in all schools and generally was considered a function of family upbringing rather than a function of religion, race, or ethnicity. Even in those schools that were and had been integrated from their beginning, undesirable behavior was associated most often with social-class status. Students were punished, but no record of punishment was kept by race. Long-term suspensions were rare.

115

Today Black students across the nation are over-represented among populations representing dropouts, long-term suspensions, and other harsh results of what on the surface would appear to be an inability to adjust to the demands of school life. Some Black students, like some students from all groups, cannot or will not conform to acceptable social standards. Often these individuals become a part of prison statistics, or they are found as a part of the drug or alcohol scene, or they abuse their lives and the lives of their fellow human beings in other damaging ways. These students, however, are generally not identifiable in statistically significant numbers. It is particularly unlikely that any one racial or ethnic group would have such over-representation without a more substantial explanation than, for example, there being something "culturally syntonic" about violence among Blacks.

In a very short historical perspective some conclusions may be drawn. Many Black parents and students feel that they are paying a penalty assessed for the desegregation of schools. Most Black students feel: (1) Theirs are the schools most likely to be closed; (2) They are the ones who suffer the greatest loss of leadership opportunity as a result of transition, (3) They are the ones most likely to be bused (and for longer distances), (4) They are the ones exposed to a strange environment with its high possibility of offering only a hostile and demeaning climate, (5) They are the ones most likely to face Black teachers who will (to them) sacrifice integrity to be accepted by their white colleagues, thereby joining in an adversary position rather than one of advocacy, and (6) They will be seen as generally "dumb" or at least as being socially and educationally inferior to their white peers. These are a few of the negative feelings harbored by a large majority of Black students as they enter desegregated situations. Many of these fears and suspicions are analogously shared by white students who are bused to predominately Black schools. However, the growing resistance by white parents and its ensuing violence tend to validate (in the minds of the Black child) the feeling that the real issue is not busing, neighborhood schools, freedom of choice, or the like, but some kind of deep-seated hatred of Blacks by whites. Very often the resentment of this and the feeling of helplessness that accompanies it explodes into acts of misconduct or violence by students who are basically quiet, reserved, law-abiding citizens. This does not excuse the behavior but may help one to understand it.

Behavior Is Behavior

Many discipline problems are discipline problems—they have no relationship to race. Indeed this statement is redundant, but we should continuously remind ourselves of its message. As complicated as it may be, many disciplinary problems simply result from the human condition—those of the students' and teachers' personalities.

Unacceptable language has always elicited a strong response from most teachers. It appears that now there is difficulty in determining what is acceptable and what is not. This is due largely to our society's more permissive attitude. "Hell" and "damn" (once strongly rejected) have gained respectability if used in a "proper context." Radio and television are no longer concerned about even the context, so students learn to use curse words "appropriately" rather than contextually. Some teachers are upset by this while others view it without alarm. Frequently students find themselves in a dilemma. To some teachers poor diction and weaknesses in syntax may make foul language among Blacks sound worse than when used by a more standard speaking person. In a more serious vein, unacceptable language is unacceptable language, but when race is injected, the entire nature of the problem is changed and a rather usual problem creates an unusual situation.

Problems caused by the human condition place full blame neither on the teacher nor on the student, although one or the other may have precipitated the incident. Teachers, when confronted by a student whose own ego needs prevent accommodation to the individual teacher's and who must save face rather than admit to error, will find themselves in an "irresistable force, immovable object" struggle. The injection of race takes the conflict off the human condition level and places it on a level beneath the dignity of that teacher. In addition it can add fuel to an age-old fire, or it can ignite the embers of a smoldering hatred.

A different kind of human condition situation can be found in the little book, *Black Misery*, by Langston Hughes. In one part Hughes speaks of Black misery as being when a white teacher tells a class that all Negroes can sing and you know that you can't carry a tune. Or Black misery is when you try to help an old white lady across the street and she thinks that you are attempting to snatch her purse. These expressions or attitudes on the part of educators represent a kind of unconscious insensitivity. Regardless of how well-intentioned the teacher, Black student reaction to insensitivity ranges from exasperation to hate. Over time such lack of feeling or awareness can result in emotional outbursts by students which, naturally, may shock the unsuspecting and painfully naive teacher. This teacher's immediate reaction might very well be voiced or felt in a negative, racially-couched attitude.

Race at no time should be injected into any situation where it doesn't belong. If it appears to be a part of a disciplinary situation, it must be removed if we are to examine the facts in an objective manner.

Teacher Behavior

There are types of teacher behavior that are direct and differ greatly from those of the insensitive, but well-meaning, teacher. At worst these are the growing number of white teachers who openly express negative attitudes toward Blacks. To the discredit of the teacher (and possibly to the profession) there are written reports by evaluation committees that carry disparaging remarks by white teachers about their Black students. This is much more widespread than one wishes to admit and elicits strong negative reactions on the part of Blacks.

A possibly more damaging teacher is the one who, only in the classroom, displays improper behavior. Derogatory statements about Blacks, ignoring Black students who seek to respond in class, presenting what would be seen as racist literature in class, and the like can force a Black student to drop out of school rather than face continual insult or, in desperation, to start breaking rules or otherwise cause trouble.

Administrators who refuse to hear the complaints of Black students and who openly call them radicals, complainers, and troublemakers appear to the student to vindicate the obnoxious teacher and blame the victim.

Black parents in this instance may not be advocates for their children for fear of retaliation by the teacher and/or principal. This only feeds the anger and feeling of injustice on the part of the Black student. This student may remain in school and may graduate but the scars remain and her/his record in school is forever blemished.

Peer Pressure

Fights among students are a rather common occurrence. Recently more of them have been designated as racial clashes. However, the next day it may prove to have been a personality clash and not a racial clash. When the basis for an altercation is race, the Black student expects to lose in one way or another.

Relationships with white peers take a toll on some Black students. Most are wary of white students and will not reach out to them for fear of rejection or other forms of hurt. When the white student reaches out she/he may find the Black student suspicious or somewhat withdrawn. These are protective devices learned by Blacks through bitter experience over the years. It is unfortunate, for many white administrators, teachers, and students have a sincere desire to befriend and live comfortably with Blacks.

It is the white student in many subtle and not-too-subtle ways who maliciously provokes the Black student that creates the most dangerous situation. The white student's loud protestation of innocence is often given credence above the mute evidence of her/his misconduct. When this occurs, it is seen as evidence of white racism. As a defense against this undesirable white student, some Blacks use the philosophy "a good offense is the best defense." This offense takes the form of loudness, bravado, picking fights, threats, extortion, and other kinds of "I'll-get-you-first" psychology. Of course some of this activity demands disciplinary action regardless of the factors that elicit it. Nonetheless, all students lose in this type of situation and treating only the symptom will not cure the ill. There are numerous kinds of peer activities that result in racial conflict and end with harsh disciplinary action—often involving the police. This possibly is the worst kind of response, though often the only possible and appropriate response. Here the white parent may be the real culprit, but the students pay for the parental crime.

General Statement

Race has become increasingly a factor in the disciplinary aspect of classroom management. For the most part, discipline problems of this nature are the result of multifarious types of resistance to school desegregation. Our children are the victims.

It is easy to inject race into situations that are completely void of any racial element. When one permits this, the stage is set for more serious problems.

Attitudes and behaviors of white administrators, teachers, and students influence Black behavior. Proper attitudes and behaviors can help the Black student develop to her/his full potential. Negative attitudes and behaviors on the part of the white school population can cause the Black student to react with violence as a result of pent-up rage. Negative reactions by whites reinforce the Black student's fears, suspicions and distrust of white society at large. The Black student who may have become a productive, contributing citizen can become instead a wasted human resource. Dropped from school, or otherwise harshly and unfairly punished, she/he may choose to drop out of life or even attempt to destroy the perceived tormentor—"Whitey." All of us lose.

Project Success Environment: One City's Approach to Learning

Marion Thompson

Director, Project Success Environment

Atlanta

Inner-city pupils—both Black and white—are consistently failing to gain an adequate education in this country's public schools. The statistical evidence is clear: inner-city children are turned off by school. They not only measure lower in I.Q. and academic achievement: they are chronically absent, disruptive in the classroom, and likely to drop out. As a group, they fall further and further behind their economically-advantaged suburban peers with each year of schooling.

For Atlanta, Georgia, the problem of inner-city education is acute; the Atlanta school system has succeeded no better than any other large system in educating this population. In Atlanta, for example, the median reading score for inner-city eighth graders is slightly below the fifth-grade level. For some time, Atlanta—like many other school systems—attempted to deal with the problem of academic underachievement in inner-city schools primarily through compensatory programs, such as teaching English-as-a-second-language or operating after-school tutorials. Like all compensatory problems, Atlanta's operated on the premise that the school itself is essentially adequate and effective and that the students who are failing are, in fact, the failures—kids who somehow just couldn't "get with" the program.

The relative ineffectiveness of the compensatory programs—at least one had a turnover of 110 percent in one year—caused some administrators in the Atlanta school system to question the concept on which they were based. Largely, this questioning led to the creation of Project Success Environment. Project Success Environment (PSE) starts with the assumption that to help the students learn, the school itself must be changed. The typical classroom is failure-oriented. All too often wrong answers, sloppy work, and disruptive behavior are what the teacher concentrates on, while good behavior and academic success are assumed to be their own reward.

120

Our public schools are designed to build successively year after year upon skills acquired by children in previous years. If at any point the child has not acquired the appropriate prerequisite skills, failure is likely. For inner-city children such failures often occur early. The project originators hypothesized that many inner-city children consistently fail because the classroom is set up so they don't experience early success; therefore, they have no successes to build on. Then, knowing only failure, they expect to fail—and they do. By restructuring the classroom, replacing the failure environment with a success environment, we have attempted to give these students successful experiences on which to build. Specifically, the project—

1. Trains teachers to be less punitive and more rewarding as they interact with students in the classroom.
2. Creates a classroom environment where students will exhibit less disruptive and more on-task behavior than students in regular classrooms.
3. Creates a classroom environment which emphasizes success and minimizes failure by building success experiences for every child into the regular classroom routine.
4. Creates a learning environment which will enable project students to achieve more academically than students in regular classes.

As the PSE staff began to construct this positive learning environment, a complete system of classroom management evolved. Eventually called the Success Technique, this system has three components: (1) a positive contingency management system designed to deliver a high rate of reinforcement (and thus success) for appropriate social and academic behaviors, (2) a classroom arrangement designed to foster small group and individualized teaching, and (3) some revision of the standard curriculum.

Reinforcement System

Teacher attitude is critical to the success of any project, so the project begins there. In a workshop held before school opens, the staff trains PSE teachers in the Success Technique, with special emphasis on the reinforcement system. All success teachers provide positive reinforcement—a tangible reward (such as check marks or tickets) coupled with verbal praise—whenever students exhibit desired behavior. Filled check-mark cards and accumulated tickets may then be exchanged for specific rewards during "trading time," a period during the day set aside especially for this purpose.

Though the system sounds simple, reinforcement is only effective when administered consistently and in specific ways. In the pre-school workshops, all PSE teachers learn to observe three basic rules. First, reinforcement must be immediate. Second, reinforcement must be accompanied by descriptive praise, which names the precise behavior being rewarded and which emphasizes that the student's own efforts are the sole cause of the reward. The teacher might say, for example, "Thank you for raising your hand, James. You have earned a ticket." Finally, only desirable behavior receives attention. This final rule is crucial to the effective functioning of a success classroom: old habits of disrupting the class to gain the teacher's attention cannot be allowed to succeed. To insure that they don't, all Success teachers are trained to use the technique of "ignore and praise" as the primary form of classroom management. When a student is disruptive or inattentive, the teacher does not deal directly with that behavior. Appearing to ignore the disruptive student, the teacher singles out a nearby student behaving in the opposite way for reward, thus cuing the desired behavior for the problem student. When the misbehaving student takes the hint and imitates the desired behavior, the teacher rewards the child immediately. Unless the student is either so disruptive that the teacher can find nothing positive to reward or is dangerous to other students, the teacher resolutely refuses to acknowledge the disruptive behavior.

Classroom Design

The PSE classroom is specifically designed both to create a framework for positive reinforcement and to make the reinforcement technique practicable. Before school opens, each Success teacher has used specific guidelines to formulate a set of rules for classroom behavior. These rules must be brief and specific, be stated positively, and be no less than three and no more than five in number. As the children enter on the first day, they see these rules prominently displayed on the walls. Then the teacher explains how she/he interprets them. From then on, each child is constantly reminded—just by looking at the walls—of the things one can—and must—do to earn rewards. Too, these same posters serve as a cue to the teacher. A large poster picturing available rewards and their token prices provides additional impetus to succeed.

Though most PSE classes are conducted in standard classrooms, they are organized for a Success Environment. The teacher can only provide immediate positive reinforcement if working with groups small enough to permit easy recognition of individual students. The classroom design makes consistent grouping feasible. Typically, a class is divided into three flexible groups. The desks are arranged in a U-shape, with each group having its own clearly defined area. This is the mastery center, where children do seatwork and receive direct instruction from the teacher. At intervals around the room are interest stations. The type and the number of interest stations vary from classroom to classroom; however, typical stations might be art, games and puzzles, library, communication, and exploratory (science). All material in each station is designed to foster specific skills, foster a high interest level, and require little teacher supervision. The materials at the stations are changed or rotated among the classrooms at least weekly. In most cases, the class time is divided into 30-minute blocks. Within a 90-minute block each group spends 30 minutes working with the teacher, 30 minutes doing seatwork, and 30 minutes at various assigned interest stations.

Curriculum

Like traditional classroom arrangements, traditional curriculum—reading, recitation, drill, homework, and weekly tests—doesn't adapt to immediate reinforcement. When the Success technique is applied to academic performance, basic curriculum must be modified to meet three criteria: (l) Each child must experience success; (2) Each child must receive work she/he can successfully do, and (3) Each child's work must be evaluated frequently and reinforced immediately. (This applies primarily to the first two-to-four weeks of school.) The standard curriculum was, therefore, modified slightly for use with the Success technique.

First, within each class the students were grouped according to reading ability, and curriculum materials were selected at levels appropriate to the three groups.

Second, an attempt was made to subdivide the curriculum in each content area to create units of work that could be completed, evaluated, and reinforced daily. For example, children were given teacher-designed skill sheets providing daily practice in each subject area. These sheets permitted immediate evaluation, feedback, and reinforcement.

The children in Project classes often started the school day with a short task requiring only that they follow directions. Commercially available perceptual-motor sheets were used along with simple tracing, design copying, and visual discrimination tasks. These order tasks were designed to get the students involved early in the day with a simple task almost certain to be completed successfully.

Day-to-Day Operation

On the first day the Success technique is introduced into the class, the teacher emphasizes good conduct by continuing to reward students primarily for following the classroom conduct rules for approximately a month. PSE students generally spend a lot more time working and a lot less time disrupting the class than students in regular classes. Four to six weeks emphasis on class rules generally produces this difference in conduct behavior.

Toward the end of the first month, too, several other things happen within the reinforcement system. First, the teacher reduces the number of rewards given out daily. To get each child involved in the system, the teacher initially tries to insure that everyone accumulates enough tokens to trade in every day. As the system catches on, however, fewer rewards become necessary. Second, the first month provides time to gradually emphasize one kind of reward more than another. The Project makes toy watches, toy jewelry, comic books, and model cars available to students at first because these all are items the students immediately relate to and find desirable. As time passes, however, activities become increasingly important, and tangible rewards are phased out.

In every classroom children vie with each other to perform certain special duties such as watering the plants, erasing the boards, making the daily attendance report, or running errands to the office. In most classes, these privileges are conferred by the teacher's whim. In PSE classes, however, they are rewards which can be earned with tokens. Further, the project has created some activity reinforcers of its own. A student may earn the responsibility of being a mini-teacher, who checks other students' work and dispenses tokens, or the privilege of leading the line to lunch, keeping the other children in order. All project-created activities allow the students to function as successful adults, thus to develop a feeling of competence and self-worth. It is not possible to overemphasize the importance of pupils modeling on warm, positive adults.

The only problem with the activity reinforcers is that no one class has enough to go around, so shortly after the technique is introduced, the project makes an activity room available to students. The activity room is stocked with a variety of games and toys—fooseball, lincoln logs, caroms, pro-soccer—chosen especially for their appeal to students, who trade their tokens for 30 minutes of free time there. Once this room is available, it becomes the basic reinforcer which backs up the token reinforcement system. By the end of the conduct phase, the reward system depends almost entirely on activities and special privileges.

From reinforcing conduct, the teacher moves to reinforcing academic behavior. Here too the teacher emphasizes success, not failure. Answers are marked "correct," instead of "wrong." And if a student has difficulty with work, the teacher doesn't fuss at the child about not listening to directions or not being prepared. The teacher stops, encourages, points the way to success, and promises to return. When dealing with both academic and social behavior, the idea is to maximize achievement and ignore failure. The teacher may begin by rewarding students for beginning work, then completion, and then, finally, mastery. Our data show if conduct has stabilized and the children are receiving work they can do which is being evaluated frequently and reinforced immediately so as to enable success, the Success technique will almost surely lead to increased academic achievement.

Project Success Environment has been a successful research endeavor and developmental effort. The statistics bear this out. Pupils have learned more. And they feel good about this learning! Their teachers enjoy teaching more! For all concerned, school has become a more pleasant place to learn and work.

Order and Justice

Classroom Control and the Search for Order

Teressa Marjorie Pratt

Elementary Principal
Waterloo School System
Waterloo, Iowa

Direction, attention, and positive reinforcement for appropriate behavior are three basic ingredients needed in the recipe to help children develop self-control. These ingredients are particularly important where teachers are working with children who have been labeled, or who have a poor self-concept brought on by years of failure and confusion in classrooms where high academic ability is prized and quiet orderly behavior is expected. Sometimes these children are classified as slow learners or emotionally disturbed. It really makes little difference what the label is because the label does not spell out the behavior in terms of what is expected of children in the classroom. Mentally retarded children will not necessarily act a certain way because of their retardation, nor can children with emotional or social problems all be expected to act the same way. Behavior is learned for the child with brain damage or for the child with perceptual problems just as it is for the normal child, and we can help all children learn to behave in a manner that minimizes disruptions and maximizes the opportunity for learning, which is the major function of the school.

Teachers will have to start by helping the children they work with learn what is expected of them each day. A lot of rules are unnecessary, but by doing the same thing every day at the same time, by having each child's desk or home base in the same place every day, and by reacting to each child in a consistent, predictable manner day in and day out, the children soon learn what is expected of them by actually performing the behavior in an appropriate way. Spelling out the consequences of children's acceptable and nonacceptable behavior is very important, for it is a first step toward giving children an opportunity to make choices of their own within the classroom structure. Knowing the consequences of behavior contributes to the effectiveness of teacher attention and reinforcement. The children should be receiving positive reinforcement, such as praise, check marks, tokens, free time, or whatever the teacher has chosen, in some consistent pattern when

127

they do what the teacher expects of them, such as facing the front of the room, working steadily at a task, working quietly or cooperating with another person. Along with this, teachers must make sure they are giving each child plenty of attention so that the individual can get needed help with work, thus preventing frustration, and so that each child can gain a feeling of self-importance. Work should certainly be provided which enables each child to meet a very high rate of success, particularly at first, and later on so that when the teacher recognizes the child's accomplishment the teacher can let the child know just what a success she/he is!

On the other hand, when behavior is inappropriate, attention and reinforcement can be withdrawn. The child may not always feel like doing as the teacher wants or may try to seek attention (from teacher or peers) in a manner that is unacceptable in the classroom setting. If the teacher has developed a hierarchy of consequences to be carried out when this occurs, it promotes rational rather than emotional encounters, and it permits some degree of choice-making on the part of the student. For instance, the child may start a temper tantrum or start shouting obscenities. The teacher can first of all withdraw her attention from the person displaying the negative behavior, while reinforcing positive behavior on the part of the remaining children. An example would be, "Joe, I like the way you went right ahead with your work even though the noise Sandra is making must be very disturbing to you." The teacher can be alert and give special praise to those who would normally react to such an outburst. Sometimes even standing in a child's line of vision while administering this praise is a good plan. If the outburst is such that it simply cannot be tolerated by the teacher and students, the child should be informed of what will happen next if the behavior doesn't stop. One must make sure, however, that the consequence is reasonable and enforceable. Then if the behavior continues, the stated action should be carried out in a matter-of-fact way. Perhaps it's removing a child from the community of the class to a private spot where the child can still continue to work and receive reinforcement if she/he starts to behave appropriately. If, however, the unacceptable behavior continues, next in a set of consequences might be a time-out room which is a room with no stimuli, with nothing for the child to do but sit. Again, the child should be informed before actually being placed there, giving the child another opportunity to make a choice about how she/he's going to act. If a child starts back to work, she/he should receive immediate reinforcement, but if the child has chosen instead to continue an obnoxious behavior, she/he might be isolated. When a child changes a behavior so that it is appropriate once again, she/he should be accepted back into the classroom community immediately, once more receiving attention and positive feedback with no grudges held over on the part of the teacher.

By consistently adhering to a plan for one's classroom, the children start behaving almost from habit as they become familiar with exactly what's expected of them in the room and the kinds of freedom they have, as well as the kinds of restrictions. They can relax and quit worrying that they will have to greet unfamiliarities each day. They can count on being successful and receiving recognition for it day after day, for they know their teacher is sensitive to their academic frustrations and the amount of time they actually can work. They are free as well from the need to mind the business of their classmates because the teacher will handle any misbehavior in the same consistent way for everyone. As the children get in the habit of acting in a manner appropriate for the classroom, it starts to carry over into other areas such as the playground, the library, and the halls. As the children start making decisions based on the ground rules established in the classroom, one can give them a chance to test their independence and self-control. The teacher can try letting them work together and reinforce their ability to cooperate. She can let them go to the library and do errands by themselves. The children can start planning an activity to present to the rest of the class, and they can start participating in group discussions and group activities where they are apt to meet frustrations and find decision-making increasingly difficult. The teacher should continue to reward them for trying and for making appropriate decisions in times of stress. If children can stay in control in these situations, they're doing all right. They can start participating in activities with other classes. If frustrations seem to be overwhelming on occasion, they can always return to their familiar structure and comfortable surroundings until they're ready to try independence once again.

Teachers can develop their own classroom structures including the kind of physical arrangement they want, the time schedule that seems most appropriate, and the ground rules for both teacher and student to follow. Within these ground rules, however, the teacher should provide for those three important ingredients—direction, attention, and a plan for giving positive reinforcement. The following questions can serve as guidelines:

How is my daily routine going to be established?

How can I set up my room so that I can provide everyone with enough attention both easily and efficiently?

What kinds of tasks am I going to provide for every child so that each one can meet a high rate of success day after day?

How am I going to positively reinforce each child on a consistent, planned basis?

What consequences am I going to build into my system in the event of unwanted behavior?

Teachers need to think carefully through their plans for the year, but also should be able to adjust when necessary. The children's behavior will be changing over the year, and teachers must be flexible enough to alter classroom expectancies in order that children will have the opportunity to use their newly gained independence and self-control. As teachers, we mustn't hold too tight, for we need to realize when it's time to let out the rein a little and demonstrate our trust and belief in children and their capabilities. They can do it with our support and encouragement!

Classroom Control and the Search for Justice

Robert B. Pratt
Associate Professor
University of Northern Iowa
Cedar Falls, Iowa

Justice in the classroom is an overriding concern of children, and its frustration the source of most discipline problems faced by teachers. Order in the classroom, on the other hand, is an overriding concern of teachers, and its frustration the source of many wasted hours of class time that could better be spent in productive learning experiences. The conflict that seems to exist between teachers and students grows out of faulty reasoning about society and the institution's role in it, particularly as it relates to classroom control and the search for justice.

All too often, educators separate the concepts of *process* and *product* in their thinking and proceed as if they were mutually exclusive and contradictory ideas. The product of "effective citizenship" as an educational goal with its subtle attributes of freedom, dignity, creativity, and self-actualization is separated from the process of "effective citizenship" and its rules, sanctions, discipline, rationality, and conformity due in the orderly attainment of educational goals. This separation of product and process is analogous to the separation of means and ends, learning and instruction, content and methodology, as well as the separation of education from the broader society it is designed to serve. Educators have been so accustomed to this dichotomy and to the compartmentalized thinking it creates that it is difficult to reconcile the process of classroom management with anything that is substantive or the least bit humanistic. Education cannot operate as an external agent of reform. At best it is a microcosm of the larger society and, as such, has the same structure and function, and therefore the same assets and liabilities, as the society it reflects.

The purpose of this article is to explore another aspect of compartmentalized thinking and faulty reasoning. It is the type of reasoning that separates the domain of law from the domain of education and both domains from the workaday world they are intended to enhance. The institutions of law and education hold out promise for solving the ills of society, but all too often they fall pathetically short in the area of workable solutions. The socialization of youth is simply too important a function in society to be the whole domain of schools and educators just as the administration of justice is too pervasive a concern to be entrusted entirely to courtrooms, lawyers, and law enforcement agents. If the practitioners of law and education can avoid their "Jekyll and Hyde" preoccupation, important perspectives from both fields can be better utilized. Used together in the classroom these perspectives combine the structure of a managed learning environment with the function of citizenship education. Law-related education in its broadest sense gives substance to this marriage and makes order and justice copartners in a union which benefits both teacher and student. The bonds of this union can be built around the use of such legal concepts as power, due process, equality, liberty, and justice.

An important area of overlap between education and law is the concept power or more appropriately, the use and abuse of power. The founders of this country respected power, but because they feared its abuse they built into the Constitution an elaborate system of checks and balances. Few teachers share a similar distrust of power, for as often as not, teachers make the law, they execute the law, and they stand in judgment over people who break the law. Used in this way power can become arbitrary and capricious—resulting in student behavior that is at best confused and at worst irresponsible and destructive. The concept *in loco parentis* does give teachers power, but it is power that must be tempered by justice, mercy, and the processes due in its even-handed application.

In classroom practice an exploration of power might involve students in the establishment of a legal system in the classroom. Together the teacher and students could explore the limits of power by coming to terms with the jurisdiction over which they have some control. The need for rules, sanctions, and procedures would then be concrete rather than abstract, and the standards of conduct reasonable rather than arbitrary. The exercise of power in this way would be explored through the determination of suitable punishments that are matched to appropriate statutes. This cooperative exercise in civics would allow students to share power and at the same time routinize and systemetize classroom management. It would also provide a vehicle that could turn future discipline problems into meaningful learning experiences.

A second area that relates education to law is the interdependent nature of justice and due process. Due process is the established procedure that gives form to justice and makes it a realizable human aspiration. In a democratic society due process assumes that when a conflict arises, individual rights are given precedence over the rights of society. In a classroom society, the rights of the individual are usually subordinated to the rights of the group. How many times are the legitimate and rightful demands of students turned aside, and how many times do these same demands return in the form of deviant behavior? If classroom management procedure is made analogous to legal procedure, justice can be served, and the many abuses of justice carried out under the guise of protecting the welfare of children can be avoided. Due process in the classroom means establishing procedures which are guided by the principles and rules of law. It is a reasonable and evenhanded procedure for handling conflict and a way of insuring that justice is served.

In classroom practice due process is little more than affording students the same rights that are guaranteed any person in a democratic society. Opportunities to explore this area arise whenever a conflict is resolved in the classroom. Was the offending student assumed innocent until proven guilty? Was the student protected against self-discrimination? Was the student able to confront accusers, call witnesses, and cross examine? Whenever the justice of an act is questioned in class, students must come to terms with the reasonableness of the processes used in its litigation.

A third area that helps form a bond between education and law is the treatment given the idea of equality in the classroom. If classroom management procedures are based on the principles and rules of law, there will be equality before the law. There is another aspect of equality which is based on the fundamental uniqueness of each individual in class. Every individual must have an equal opportunity to develop her/his uniqueness. This gives substance to the dictum that teachers must meet the needs of the people they serve. Equality implies a dual responsibility for teachers. In a legal sense it involves the development, enunciation, and consistent application of reasonable classroom procedures, sanctions, and rules. In a professional sense, it involves substantive educational programs and teaching behavior that help students develop to their fullest potential.

In classroom practice the exploration of equality might involve the study of contractual relationships. Individualized instruction implies a contractual relationship between the teacher and students. Teachers, as educational specialists, have contractual obligations to develop the uniqueness of each individual in class. Students, in turn, have certain contractual obligations as learners. As learners become specialists themselves, they, too, enter into contractual arrangements in order to receive just return due to their specialization and in accordance with the economic realities of the division of labor within our highly technical society.

The fourth link between education and law is liberty. It is difficult to discuss liberty without also describing the responsibilities that accompany it. Without responsibility liberty becomes sheer license that impedes humankind's individual and collective right to exist. In our society the First Amendment strikes a balance between liberty and license. A similar balance should be struck in the society of the classroom. Freedom, dignity, creativity, and self-actualization do not grow out of chaos; rather, they come from order and its foundation in the rules, sanctions, discipline, conformity, and rationality that make them operational. The former virtues emanate from the search for knowledge and the intellectual needs of students. The latter virtues emanate from the search for justice and the equally important and interrelated moral needs of students.

In classroom practice the exploration of liberty can involve all three domains of student response. In the cognitive domain the attributes of liberty are woven through current events and the subject fields of history, economics, political science, anthropology, and sociology. In the affective domain questions of fundamental human liberty provide spring boards for tough-minded value clarification exercises. Many times the legal issues treated in the classroom are not between right and wrong behavior but between two seemingly equal and correct behaviors that are in conflict. Problem-solving and conflict resolution develop the students' inquiry and critical thinking skills.

The final and most pervasive bond connecting education and law is justice. Although justice cannot be separated from the other bonds and linkages, it deserves mention in its own right as a vital component of any citizenship education program. As a value, justice is distinct from all other values because it provides a criterion against which power, due process, equality, and liberty are measured. Justice measures the reasonableness of these other law-related concepts in terms of universal principles rather than by expediency or conventional morality. Morality cannot be instilled through the imposition of values but rather through the process teachers and students use in determining the rightness or wrongness of behavior. This invokes the type of choice and decision-making that enables the resolution of conflict, which is the mediation between equally "correct" solutions and the application of the justice to the decisions that give meaning to life.

If classroom management is conscientiously related to the spirit as well as the letter of the law, it will be reasonable. Reasonable conduct does not violate justice but enhances it. Reasonable conduct on the part of teachers will make classroom control and the search for justice a compatible and realistic goal for education.

A Child's Garden
of Law and Order

June L. Tapp

Program Director and Senior
Social Psychologist, American Bar Association

Every country, whatever its political and economic philosophy, must produce individuals who are both independent and compliant: citizens who will conform to the socially prescribed rules of behavior and accept them as their own values. But neither the proliferation of programs nor a recitation of rules can assure these goals.

Legal theorists and psychologists have increasingly realized that the internalization of values, not the threat or risk of specific legal penalties, is responsible for compliance with the law and social rules. To understand what makes people obey these norms—or deviate from them—one must begin from the perspective of the normal citizen, not from the perspective of the criminal.

Many researchers dislike the terms *obedience* and *compliance* because of their strong moral connotations. Stanley Milgram's experiment on conditions of disobedience, for example, made the point that blind obedience to an authority is destructive; he concluded that too few persons behave autonomously. But the study of legal socialization does not necessarily have as a premise that compliance itself is good or bad; the study is concerned with the ways in which individuals learn the rules and norms of their society.

Across. A good way to achieve this understanding is to observe children in different cultures, inquiring: 1) whether the same authority figures are important across nations; 2) whether people throughout the world share notions about the legitimacy of rule-breaking and the nature and function of rules and laws; 3) whether children develop in similar ways in their attitudes toward legitimacy, morality and justice.

Robert Hess, Leigh Minturn and I conducted a cross-cultural study to investigate common features in the development of compliance. Working with us in Europe and Asia were field teams under the direction of Vasso Vassiliou, Svend Skyum-Nielsen, B. Kuppuswamy,

Reprinted with permission from *Psychology Today*, December 1970. Copyright © Ziff-Davis Publishing Company.

Marcello Cesa-Bianchi, and Akira Hoshino. We studied almost 5,000 middle-school children in seven cultures in Greece, Denmark, India, Italy, Japan and the United States (black and white). Choosing children of ages 10 to 14 is consistent with other investigations that show this period to be critical in moral and legal understanding. Lawrence Kohlberg, for example, reported substantial correlations between the moral views a person has at this age and those he holds in adulthood. Preadolescence, moreover, is the incubating period: the time when crime rates begin to go up and many children become sexually active. Most important, this period precedes the adolescent spurt in which children begin to make ideological, political and occupational decisions.

Questions. We gave a battery of tests to all of these children and then, for more intensive study, we interviewed a random sample of 406 children, roughly 60 in each culture. These included 20 from each of three grades (fourth, sixth and eighth), equally divided in turn by social class (professional or working) and sex.

In the interview we asked 79 open-ended questions, including these basic ones:

1) *What is a rule?*
2) *What is a law?*
3) *What is the difference between a rule and a law?*
4) *What would happen if there were no rules at all?*
5) *What is a fair rule?*
6) *Are there times when it might be right to break a rule?*
7) *Who can make you follow a rule?*

Norms. Before anyone can understand a system's legal order, he must have a concept of a rule and a law, and their differences. Cross-culturally, children believed that the nature and function of rules and laws were the same. When we asked: *What is a rule?* and *What is a law?*, children in all seven cultures defined both, using the same three functional categories:

1) *Prescriptive*—a general guideline, a neutral regulation. "It's a guideline to follow," said a U.S. white eighth-grade girl. "Just—well, you just follow it."

2) *Prohibitive*—a guideline that forbids behavior. An American white sixth-grade boy explained: "A rule, to me, it's more like a restriction that tells you what you can do and what you can't do . . . well, like a rule at school is that you can't chew gum or you'll get in trouble."

3) *Beneficial*—a guideline with a rational social or personal reason for existing. "It is what is necessary for the group life," reported a Japanese sixth-grade girl, "and—if it is kept by all—the group activity goes in order."

Although there was some variation between cultures in the frequency with which these three functions were cited, in five of seven cultures children's characterizations of rules and laws were parallel. We found that the *prescriptive* quality was the most widely recognized. In all seven cultures it was a typical answer (defined here as at least 20 percent). Older children were more inclined to stress prescription;

they gave fewer *don't know* responses, reflecting their newly increased knowledge and social awareness. In five of seven cultures, *prohibitive* was the second most typical answer for rules; this was true in six of seven for laws.

Most children, then, saw the *functions* of laws and rules as the same: they regarded both as special norms that guide behavior and require obedience. A key finding was that the concept of coercion was noticeably absent from their answers. The children focused on the content and purpose of rules, not on punishment and authority. This reluctance to recognize coercion suggests, as many legal scholars and social scientists maintain, that coercion and force do not insure obedience to the law, and that they are not the defining quality of all things legal or rulelike.

Although children thought that rules and laws perform in the same way, they saw differences between them when they were asked. Not surprisingly, in six out of seven cultures they saw rules as more specific and laws as more general. This distinction, however, was more a matter of sphere, scope, or jurisdiction than function. For example, the children's answers reflected the popular notion that *laws* had a government or state implication, whereas *rules* were nongovernmental in nature. This suggests that understanding the function of state law is part of a larger enterprise of understanding the function of rules and laws in other institutions.

We found marked developmental similarities across cultures. Regardless of country, the older a child was, the more likely he was to impute specificity to rules and generality to laws. With experience and age children learn that it is permissible to use the terms *laws* and *the law* in speaking of the rules that are more comprehensive and general.

Shadow. What if there were no rules at all? Children in all countries predicted the same result: without rules there would be chaos, disorder and anarchy. In addition, children in five cultures foresaw violence, crime and personal gain as outcomes.

As children saw it, the essential purpose of rules was to order man's relationships in the world: to facilitate human interaction. The children also seemed to have a fearful, distrusting view of mankind. Without rules, they said, man's natural evil would take over—anarchy, violence and greed would win out. One fourth-grade, white American boy represented the view taken by most of the children: "Well, it would be a lot of disorganizing in the world. You know, people would go around killing each other. It wouldn't be organized, and there wouldn't be any school or anything like that." Said one Danish boy: "The whole world would be under chaos."

Age and experience apparently darken a child's view of human nature. Older children in all but two of the countries studied were more likely than younger ones to say that disorder and personal gain would prevail if rule and law failed. "Everyone would do what he wanted," said an Italian sixth-grader. A more sophisticated Italian eighth-grader explained: "Life would not have a logical direction."

Because socialization aims to produce individuals who will want to comply, children may be learning explicitly—from parents and other authorities—that chaos and conflict would ensue if we had no rules. In any case few children can imagine a world without laws and few dare suggest that good might survive without them. Rules and laws control and deter man's irrational, aggressive and egoistic motives.

Justice. Given this acceptance of rules how do children distinguish among them? Are all rules fair, or are some more fair than others? To ascertain the essence of justice, we asked: *What is a fair rule?*

In six out of seven cultures, children could separate the concept of rule from that of a fair rule. Only in one country—India—was *All rules are fair* the typical response. Interestingly, in all seven cultures fewer than five percent defined a fair rule as one created by an authority; the fact that a rule was made by the powers-that-be did not necessarily mean that it was just.

Although there was some variation across countries in definitions of rule fairness, two components stood out in the children's responses:

1) *Consensus.* A primary response in five cultures was that a fair rule is one with which everyone agrees. American children gave us some good examples of this answer: "Everybody likes it," said a white fourth-grade girl, and, "When somebody suggests a rule and everybody thinks it's right, then it's fair," said a black eighth-grade boy.

2) *Equality.* A typical answer in four cultures was that a fair rule is one everyone must obey, one that affects everyone without favoritism. As one U.S. white fourth-grade girl observed: "We should both get yelled at for talking, but it's not fair for one person to get yelled at." A U.S. black eighth-grade boy defined a fair rule as: "a rule that would apply to everyone fairly and it wouldn't put one person out and another person in."

Among U.S. children a third answer was characteristic: both blacks and whites emphasized the *rational-beneficial* dimension of fairness. A fair rule, they said, is one that is reasonable and useful. In the words of a fourth-grade black boy: "Because it is a good thing and it is helping you from getting hurt."

Demands. In five cultures, as children grew older they were less likely to believe that all rules are fair; and in six cultures were more likely to think that equality is basic to the concept of fairness. With age, they also question adults more and make increased demands for respect and reciprocity.

There are important implications for legal systems in the fact that children see a fair system as one that embraces participatory and cooperative efforts among equals. Justice requires consensual participation, impersonal distribution, and shared power.

Violation. We further probed attitudes about the function and fairness of rules by asking: *Are there times when it might be right to break a rule?* Only in two cultures were children most likely to reply that *no* rule was breakable; in five, children readily accepted the possibility of rule-breaking. Although in all cultures their reasons varied, in five cultures children thought that rule-breaking was permissible for higher moral reasons—that is, if the rule were less important than the situation or reason for breaking it. This answer, based on the *morality of circumstances*, was well expressed by a U.S. white eighth-grader: "Well, it depends on what's going on. If it's a matter of life and death or you know something pretty important, then it's all right. But the rule should be followed as much as possible." Or, as a more imaginative child expounded: "When you're hungry and you go in the store and steal something. When you need money, like for someone kidnapped someone in your family and he stole it from the bank, paid the ransom and you try to pay the money back to the bank. Money and food could be replaced but the person in life couldn't."

Only in one country, Italy, was the *morality of the rule* itself the dominant response; that is, children felt freer to break a rule they thought was intrinsically unfair.

Substantial numbers of children, then, recognized that rules and laws are not infallible or absolute. They accepted just and legitimate reasons for transgressions. As they grew older, children in at least five countries increasingly accepted the legitimacy of breaking rules with moral cause, findings consistent with work on moral development by Jean Piaget and Lawrence Kohlberg.

Authority. Finally, to determine what authority figures were important in socializing children into compliance, we asked: *Who can make you follow a rule?* Father, mother, teacher and policeman emerged as the major authorities for children.

In six of the seven cultures, parents were most able to make children follow rules; there was variation as to which parent came first, reflecting different norms about who does the punishing in the home. In only one country, Japan, the teacher ranked higher than parents; everywhere else, the teacher generally followed parents in ranking of effective rule enforcers. The number of children who said policemen made them follow rules was comparatively lower, but substantial percentages nominated this symbol of law enforcement. The police ranked at least fourth in all cultures except in India, where children mentioned government officials instead.

Parents, being closest to children and most familiar to them, were, as we would expect, most able to make them obey; the distant policeman and official were not as effective in gaining compliance. This finding suggests, along with other research in psychology and law, that affiliative, nurturant strategies—rather than punitive ones—are most effective in inducing compliance and assuring the stability of systems. Persuasion, not coercion, is more likely to be linked with compliance and independence.

Hope. Considering the range of countries and the diversity of political, religious and economic styles represented in our survey, it is remarkable that there should be such similarities across the seven cultures. The children see rules and laws as performing equivalent functions in the ordering of human conduct. They recognize the need for order in human affairs, and the role that rules and laws play in providing that order. They want a fair system—one that emphasizes equality and consensus. And they agree that with good reason or moral justification, rules could legitimately be violated.

Such striking convergences across such divergent nations are, I like to think, a good sign. The common trends of child development and the socialization goals that transcend nationality suggest that the shared values throughout our world are more compelling than diverse ideologies would imply. If these children's wisdom could be maintained into adulthood, there might be a better chance for freedom and justice within a world society, which after all is the message of law.